Power Hapkido
Essential Techniques

Grandmaster Myung Yong Kim
Founder of Jin Jung Kwan Hapkido

총재님 김명용

진중관 합기도

Copyright © 2011

DISCLAIMER

THIS BOOK REGARDING THE MARTIAL ART OF KOREAN HAPKIDO IS PROVIDED SOLELY FOR INFORMATIONAL PURPOSES AND NO OTHER PURPOSE. THE AUTHOR, MYUNG YONG KIM, CONTRIBUTORS, PUBLISHER, AND DISTRIBUTORS OF THIS BOOK DISCLAIM ANY LIABILITY OR RESPONSIBILITY FOR PERSONAL INJURY, DAMAGE, OR LOSS IN CONNECTION WITH THE CONTENT OF THIS BOOK. FURTHER, THE SUITABILITY, APPROPRIATENESS, OR LEGALITY REGARDING THE USAGE OF THE CONTENT OF THIS BOOK IN ANY PARTICULAR SITUATION OR UNDER THE LAWS OF AN APPLICABLE JURISDICTION ARE FURTHER DISCLAIMED. ALL EXPRESS AND IMPLIED WARRANTIES ARE DISCLAIMED INCLUDING BUT NOT LIMITED TO THE IMPLIED WARRANTY OF MERCHANTABILITY AND THE IMPLIED WARRANTY OF FITNESS FOR A PARTICULAR PURPOSE.

Martial arts practice is a potentially dangerous activity for all individuals involved. Injuries might include, but are not limited to, muscle soreness; scrapes; cuts; bruises; dislocations; broken bones; nerve damage; torn ligaments, tendons, and muscles; and internal organ injury. In rare cases, participants might suffer cardiac arrest; stroke; serious and permanently disabling physical injuries; and death. Any individual intending to participate in martial arts practice should first consult with a qualified health-care professional regarding the individual's suitability for intense physical and aerobic, martial-arts activity.

Any individual learning a martial art should proceed only under the instruction and guidance of a qualified, trained expert in the field. Usage of martial arts techniques upon another individual can result in serious and disabling injuries and in some cases death.

Any usage of martial arts for self-defense should be conducted only as authorized by applicable criminal and civil laws. Legally unjustifiable use of martial arts techniques may result in criminal prosecution and/or civil liability.

Table of Contents

Intentionally
Left
Blank

INTRODUCTION

Hapkido is a gentleman's martial art. It is the art of: expending just enough energy necessary to subdue an opponent; perceiving an impending attack and countering it so the fight ends before it starts; and redirection and circular motion that allows a weaker person to defend against a stronger opponent.

A Hapkido practitioner is a man reluctant to engage in battle. He will use Hapkido as a last resort to resolve a problem. Nevertheless, he is a person who does not hesitate to use it should he deem it necessary.

With the plethora of different styles out there, and especially with the popularity of the ground and pound fighting styles of current mixed martial arts, we offer Hapkido as a viable alternative for those seeking less violent styles. If you are looking to take on the meanest, toughest looking man in a bar and start a fight, we suggest you look elsewhere for instruction.

Having said that, for those who are sincere in wanting to learn a defensive fighting system which allows you to protect yourself and your loved ones in a hostile situation, we believe Hapkido can be of help to you.

In this book you will learn escapes, counters, and submissions to different forms of attacks. Not everyone will attack with a sucker punch nor will everyone try a takedown to the ground. Some may grab your wrist to pull you in. Others may pin you by the sleeves of your jacket to strike you with a headbutt. Others may grab you by the front of your shirt ready to pound your face in with a hammerfist. Hapkido effectively teaches how to defend against such attacks and more. With diligent practice, the techniques will become second nature and you will be able to quickly respond to perceived threats. But this will occur only with practice, so practice hard and practice frequently.

After much deliberation, Grandmaster Kim selected the techniques in this book which he felt were the essentials of Hapkido. He chose the techniques that he felt would help build a solid foundation from which further progress can be made. This book was written so that both beginners and experienced individuals alike can easily follow along and learn the techniques. The step by step instructions with the corresponding pictures should facilitate the beginner in learning the techniques. Likewise, this book should serve as a reference guide to the more experienced individual. We tried to include as many pictures as possible with close ups of important points in the techniques.

It is our sincere desire that readers will learn much from this book and use it as a means to confidently defend himself.

Email: jjkhapkido@yahoo.com
Website: jjkhapkido.com
Written Correspondence:
   JJK Hapkido
   P.O. Box 79575
   Houston, Tx 77279

Grandmaster Myung Yong Kim

"Hapkido has been the one true passion in my life. It was this passion that led to the founding of Jin Jung Kwan and its subsequent dissemination throughout South Korea and the rest of the world. This single passion has afforded me the luxury of teaching many brilliant students and passing on the knowledge of what I consider to be an exceptional martial art. Recently, there has been a major development in martial arts with the introduction of mixed martial arts. While I applaud this development, I believe that Hapkido is the foundation from which other art forms can be built upon. It is this solid unshakeable spirit of Hapkido that I wish to pass on to you with this

manual. This book contains the basic, fundamental skills of early, original Hapkido that many generations of students have successfully learned and used confidently. I truly hope that this book will guide you to a deeper appreciation and understanding of Hapkido".

Grandmaster Myung Yong Kim

Houston, Texas   2011

GM Kim Biographical Timeline

1959 –at the age of 17, Myung Yong Kim started training Hapkido at Seung Moo Kwan School under Grandmaster Ji Han Jae.

1964 – receives his 4th Dan from the Korea Hapkido Association (K.H.A.).

1965 – teaches at the Sung Dong dojang in Korea.

1967 – receives his 5th Dan. Founds Jin Jung Kwan Hapkido.

1968 – Hapkido instructor in the military camp at Wang Shim Ri.

1969 –officially opens the second Jin Jung Kwan dojang under the KHA.

1970 – becomes 6th Dan under the KHA.

1971 –December 26th , Myung Yong Kim receives 7th Dan from the KHA.

1973 – opens third Jin Jung Kwan dojang in Sung Dong Korea.

1974 – opens fourth Jin Jung Kwan dojang.

1975 –Grandmaster Myung Yong Kim emigrates to United States of America and opens a Hapkido dojang in Chicago, Illinois. Grandmaster Chang Soo Lee takes over Jin Jung Kwan in Korea from Grandmaster Myung Yong Kim.

1976 – Grandmaster Kim moves to Fullerton in Chicago.

GM Kim Biographical Timeline

1977 – in September, Grandmaster Kim returns to Korea. In Seoul, South Korea, he opens Jin Jung Kwan headquarters in Myun Mok Dong.

1980 – in May, he returns to Chicago and opens another dojang.

1982 – moves down to Houston, Texas.

1983 – in March, he opens Kim's Hapkido dojang in Houston, Texas.

1993 – he is promoted to 9th Dan by the Korea Hapkido Federation.

2011 – Grandmaster Myung Yong Kim still resides in Houston, Texas and actively instructs students in the art of Hapkido.

Original Masters of Hapkido

Grandmaster Myung Yong Kim on the 2nd row, all the way on the right. Sitting down in the front row, starting from the left side: (Song Ju Won, Kwon Tae Mahn, Kim Young Hwan, Ji Han Jae, Hwang Duk Ku, Myung Kwang Sik, Lee Tae Joon, and Kim Jong Tek).

Hwang Duk Koo, **GM Myung Yong Kim**, Kwang Sik Myung,
Ee Hun Oo.

GM Kim executing what he likes to
call "the million dollar technique!"

Grandmaster Kim holding up weighted barbell with his mouth (unknown date).

GM Kim executing a technique against 2 opponents.

GM Kim instructing a student on short stick defense.

GM Kim practicing sparring with a partner outdoors.

GM Kim on the left during a sparring demonstration in Korea.

GM Kim 2nd from the left with GM Chang Soo Lee next to him.

GM Kim instructing his students outdoors. Unknown date.

GM Kim all the way in the back center, instructing students during a special weekend outdoor session.

GM Kim demonstrating arm locks against two opponents.

GM Kim in Chicago, standing in front of his Hapkido school.

GM Kim in his Houston school.

Seminar held in France. GM Choi Kil Bong (JJK Germany), GM Yon Seung Ho, GM **Myung Yong Kim**, GM Chang Soo Lee, Master Raphael Couet (JJK France).

GM Kim seated in the center with students from JJK France.

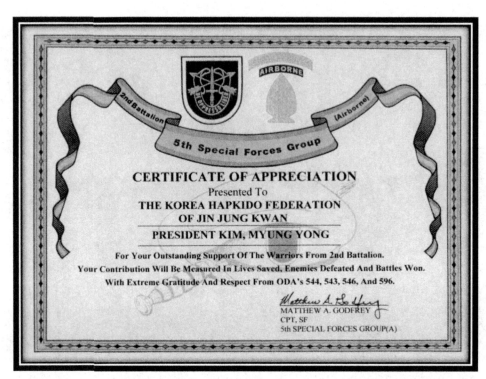

CERTIFICATE OF APPRECIATION

Presented To

THE KOREA HAPKIDO FEDERATION
OF JIN JUNG KWAN

PRESIDENT KIM, MYUNG YONG

For Your Outstanding Support Of The Warriors From 2nd Battalion.
Your Contribution Will Be Measured In Lives Saved, Enemies Defeated And Battles Won.
With Extreme Gratitude And Respect From ODA's 544, 543, 546, And 596.

MATTHEW A. GODFREY
CPT, SF
5th SPECIAL FORCES GROUP(A)

Certificate of Appreciation from the 5th Special Forces Group

CERTIFICATE OF APPRECIATION

Presented To

THE KOREA HAPKIDO FEDERATION
OF JIN JUNG KWAN

PRESIDENT KIM, MYUNG YONG

For Your Outstanding Support Of The Warriors From 2nd Battalion.
Your Contribution Will Be Measured In Lives Saved, Enemies Defeated And Battles Won.
With Extreme Gratitude And Respect From ODA's 544, 543, 546, And 596.

MATTHEW A. GODFREY
CPT, SF
5th SPECIAL FORCES GROUP(A)

16

GM Kim at a seminar in GM Rhoades' JJKHKD
School in Missouri.

GM Kim and GM Rhoades, observing
students during their promotional test.

GM Kim with GM Rhoades (above).
GM Kim with several of the Special Forces guys. (below)

Seminar in Tennessee at Master Garland's school.

Meaning of Hap Ki Do

"Hap" means unity.

"Ki" signifies power and energy.

"Do" means the way.

Hapkido teaches its practitioners to:

1) Be humble.

2) Be brave.

3) Never compromise with injustice.

4) Never initiate a confrontation.

Purpose of Practicing Hapkido :

1) A practical, legal self-defense system for dangerous situations.

2) Develop physical strength by training the body and spirit while also cultivating a sound mind.

3) Develop patience within one's own personality.

What You Should Know Before Starting A Hapkido Workout

1. Proper Stretching, warm up, and cool down exercises.

2. Consult a Physician before beginning rigorous exercise.

3. This book is written with beginners in mind with many photos and descriptions and can also be used as a reference guide for current practitioners.

4. Although there are many Hapkido "Kwans", the techniques shown in this book are the basics that any Hapkido student should know before attaining their 1st degree black belt.

5. Practice techniques with a partner but do so slowly and deliberately.

6. Never joke around, laugh, or lose concentration while practicing. Lack of concentration can lead to unintended injuries.

7. These techniques are meant for adults and are not intended for children. If you choose to teach your children, be sure you carefully supervise them.

8. When you practice, practice hard. Do not be lazy. The harder you practice, the better you will be.

Dan Jun Ho Hup
단전호흡
(Abdominal Breathing Exercise)

Hapkido has a unique abdominal breathing technique called "Dan Jun Ho Hup". The purpose of this exercise is to develop "Ki", power stored in the region of the lower abdomen. The "Ki" is the source of tremendous power that emanates from within. Muscle strength alone will only take you halfway to your destination. It is the Dan Jun power that will carry you all the way through. By practicing Dan Jun Ho Hup on a daily basis, a person is able to tap into this great sea of power and use it in a fight to defeat his opponent(s).

The Dan Jun, located about 1.25 – 1.5 inches below the naval, is the most fundamental of the Dan Juns. This is called the Ha-Dan Jun. There are two other Dan Juns called Joong-Dan Jun and Sang-Dan Jun. The Joong-Dan Jun is located near the solar plexus and controls the five senses and the emotions. Sang-Dan Jun is located on the face between the eyebrows and controls our logic, memory, and ability to analyze. The progression of the Ki through the three different Dan Juns follows the path of the individual's growth through life.

As infants we are mainly concerned with the Ha-Dan Jun, the abdominal breathing. If you haven't noticed, observe an infant's abdomen next time and you will see that he breathes solely with his abdomen. Also, if you have ever wondered how an infant so tiny could have such strong grip and pull strength, it is because of the Ha-Dan Jun.

Dan Jun Ho Hup
단전호흡
(Abdominal Breathing Exercise)

When the infant becomes a child, the Ki moves into the Joong-Dan Jun in the solar plexus. The Ki then moves into the Sang-Dan Jun when individuals mature and ends up causing much of the stress in modern life. Most adults overuse the Sang-Dan Jun trying to juggle family responsibilities, work, and friends.

This lack of balance between the Dan Juns causes a person to weaken and become ill. However, by using Dan Jun Ho Hup exercises, one can cultivate the Ki power back into the Ha-Dan Jun and maintain good health and utilize great energy.

** When you begin this exercise, the starting position is ALWAYS with your feet about shoulder width apart and your hands at your waist, fingers straight and wide open.

** At the end of the exercise, breathe out slowly, stand up, and bring your hands back to the starting position.

Dan Jun Ho Hup #1
Front

1) Begin in the starting position.

2) Slowly breathe in deep through your nose and hold it in.

3) Bend your knees slightly and at the same time move your hands upward and forward at a 45 degree angle. Keep your fingers wide open, straight, and fully tensed.

4) Once your thumbs reach your eye level put final power down to your "Dan Jun" and tilt your hands in a downward angle so that your thumbs are parallel to the floor.

5) Slowly breathe out through your mouth as you stand back up and bring your hands back to the starting position.

6) Repeat this exercise for a total of 5 times.

** Keep your arms shoulder width apart.

** Most important: practice pushing the pressure (power) down to your lower stomach (Dan Jun). Do not have the pressure up in your face, neck, or chest.

Each of the "Dan Jun" exercises should last between 5-8 seconds to complete.

The next two pages shows the exercise being done from the side profile and the front profile. Pictures are shown in sequential order going from left to right.

Dan Jun Ho Hup #1 – Front

Dan Jun Ho Hup #1 - Front

Dan Jun Ho Hup #2 - Down

1) Begin in the starting position.

2) Slowly breathe in deep through your nose and hold it in.

3) Bend your knees slightly and slowly push down your hands in front of your body (palms should be facing your body)

4) Push your hands down, fully extending your arms all the way. At this point, you should have put final power to your "dan jun", making it very tight.

5) As you stand back up, slowly exhale through your mouth as you bring your hands back slowly to the starting position.

6) Repeat the exercise for a total of 5 times.

• Arms and fingers should be tense throughout this movement.

• Make sure you inhale through your nose and exhale through your mouth.

• Make your movement slow and steady, allowing approximately 5-8 seconds for the movement.

• Push your pressure (power) down to your "Dan Jun". Make sure you do not keep the pressure up in your face, neck, or chest.

• Pictures are shown going in sequential order from the left to the right.

Dan Jun Ho Hup #2 - Down

Dan Jun Ho Hup #3 - Up

1) Begin in the starting position.

2) Slowly breathe in deep through your nose and hold it in.

3) Bend your knees slightly.

4) Drag your hands up (palms up) along the sides of your body.

5) Once your hands reach the shoulder tilt your head up and turn the hands so the thumbs are facing each other and continue raising them until the arms are fully extended. Think of lifting an object overhead.

6) Slowly breathe out through your mouth as you stand back up and bring your hands back to the starting position.

7) Repeat this exercise for a total of 5 times.

** Arms and fingers should be fully tensed.

** Exercise should take approximately 5-8 seconds.

Dan Jun Ho Hup #3 - Up

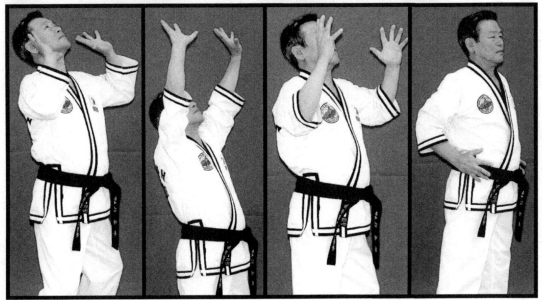

Dan Jun Ho Hup #4 - Side

1) Begin in the starting position.

2) Slowly breathe in deep through your nose and hold it in.

3) Bend your knees slightly and raise your hands to your shoulder level (palms should be facing up).

4) Turn your palms outward and push it out to the side, extending your arms out fully.

5) Once fully extended, turn your hands inward (backs of your hands should be facing each other now) and draw in your arms slowly towards the front of your body.

6) When your arms get approximately shoulder width apart twist your hands back so that the palms are facing each other.

7) Slowly breathe out through your mouth as you stand back up and bring your hands back to the starting position.

8) Repeat this exercise for a total of 5 times.

Dan Jun Ho Hup #4 - Side

HAPKIDO KICKS
단식 족술 (Single Kicks)
(dan shick jok sool)

Hapkido utilizes a variety of kicks by using parts of the foot to attack and suppress an opponent. They should be practiced daily to increase power, accuracy, and form.

Hapkido kicks are used in both close fighting and distance fighting. Some of the major targets on the human body are the ribs, face, and thighs; however, Hapkido kicks are also practiced to target some of the more vital parts of the human body to inflict destructive damage. Therefore, it is vital to practice the kicks for accuracy.

The power in Hapkido kicks comes from the entire body, especially the waist. Just as boxers bend and then fully extend the arms to hit their target(s), Hapkido kicks generate power in much the same fashion. With proper training and practice, the kicks can be effectively utilized in many different fighting situations.

The Fighting Stance: feet are approximately shoulder width apart, right foot back approximately 1-1.5 ft. Back of the heel should be slightly lifted and the arms are up with elbows down.

Practice the kicks 10 times each, executing them with full power and speed every single time.

Rising Stretching Kick
뒤꿈치 차올리기
(dwi goom chi – cha – ohl lee gi)

1. Begin in the fighting stance.

2. Square off your body to the front as you bring your right forearm above your head in a head-block.

3. Keeping your leg straight and toes pulled back, raise it straight up as high and fast as you can.

Rising Stretching Kick

4. Continue to bring the kicking leg up. As you do this, lift your left heel for balance.

Ideally, you should be able to touch the front part of your thigh to your chest.

Use this kick as a good stretching kick to loosen up your legs.

Inside Crescent Kick
안다리 차기
(ahn da ri – cha gi)

1. Begin in the fighting stance.

2. Square off your upper body to the front as you execute an inside forearm block with your right arm.

3. Using the inside part of your foot, with the toes pulled back, bring it up in a counter clockwise circular motion.

Inside Crescent Kick

4. Raise up your left heel as you bring your right foot up as high as you can, still continuing in the circular motion.

5. Be sure and keep your kicking leg straight. Kick through your target.

6. Continue through the target and bring your foot down and back into the fighting stance.

Intended target(s): side of the face and the side of the chest.

Outside Crescent Kick
바깥다리 차기
(ba gaht da ri – cha gi)

1. Begin in the fighting stance.

2. Keeping your leg straight and toes pulled back, swing your foot in a clockwise circular motion.

3. Raise your leg as quickly and as high as you can. Slightly raise your left heel as you bring your kicking leg up.

4. Continue in the circular motion, kicking through the target with the outside blade of your foot.

5, Bring your foot down and back in the fighting stance. Your target is to the face, chin, and chest.

Side Kick
옆차기
(yup cha gi)

1. Begin in the fighting stance.

2. Keeping your kicking leg loose, bring your knee up lightly and quickly to your waist height.

3. Pivot on your left foot so the toes are pointing away from you. Twist your body to the left as you bring your right foot up to execute the kick. Power of the kick comes from straightening out your body and leg. You do this by pulling back your upper back as you push in your glute.

4. Put full power into the kick right before hitting the target. Toes are pulled back and the heel slightly higher than the toes. Your body should be linear.

Side Kick – (side profile)

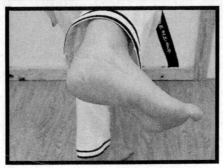

Jok Do Kick – (front profile)
족기 지르기
(jok gi – ji roo gi)

1. Begin in the fighting stance.

2. Square off your body to the front while you execute an inside forearm block.

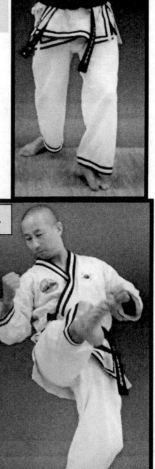

3,4. Keeping your leg loose, bring your knee up to waist height. Snap your foot (toes pointed and twisted to the right) at the target, which is the groin area. Be sure to put your hip into the kick and lean back slightly. The power is generated from the speed, so be sure to execute this kick quickly and accurately.

Jok Do Kick – (side profile)

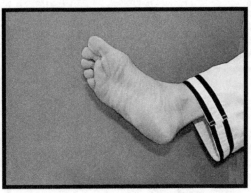

Shin Kick
안다리 차넣기
(ahn da ri – cha nuh ki)

1. Begin in the fighting stance.

2. Move your left foot so that the toes are pointing out while you execute a left hand head block and a down block with your right hand.

3,4. Now bring your right leg out in a downward angle with your toes pulled back and pointing outward. Snap the kick by bending at the knee and then bringing the rest of the leg out and down onto the opponent's shin.

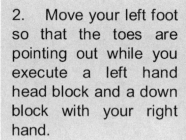

Again, this kick is done in close proximity to the opponent. It should be done in one quick motion. Be sure to lean back slightly and put your hip into the kick for added power.

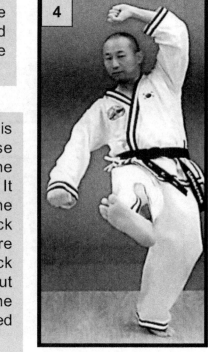

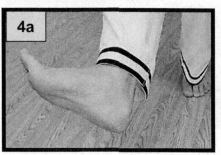

Turn Shin Kick
뒤꿈치 차돌리기
(dwi goom chi – cha – dohl lee gi)

1. Begin in the fighting stance.

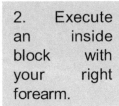

2. Execute an inside block with your right forearm.

3. Turn your leg inward to make a wide circular clockwise motion.

You are kicking with your heel to the opponent's shin. Your toes will be pulled back to assist in kicking with the heel.

4. Bring your foot out and wide to your left side first, then bend your left knee slightly and bring your kicking leg in the opposite direction, striking the opponent on the shin with your heel.

Turn Shin Kick

5. Again, speed is essential when executing this kick. This kick can be used to strike the inner thigh, knee cap, or the shin of your opponent.

Be sure to kick through the target. Don't just stop your kick at the target. Drive through the target. .

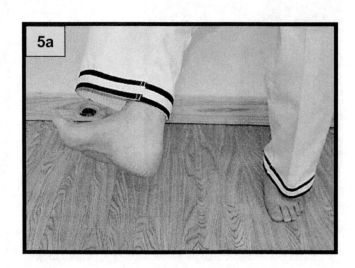

Thigh Kick
뒤꿈치로 넓적다리 차기
(dwi goom chi row — nup jjuck da ri — cha gi)

1. Begin in the fighting stance.

2. Execute an inside forearm block.

3. Bring your right leg out to your side up to waist height. Tilt your body to the right slightly as you bring your leg up.

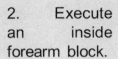

NOTE: To locate the pressure point on the thigh, stand straight with feet together and your hands straight down your side. Where your middle finger is at is where the thigh pressure point is.

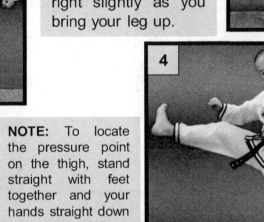

4,5. With your toes pulled back, bend your right knee, bringing down your heel at a downward angle onto your opponent's thigh. Be sure to bend your left knee while executing this kick in order to help facilitate the kick. This kick is powerful and can bring down your opponent.

The body positioning of this kick may feel and look awkward at first but with practice you will come to enjoy this kick.

Jok Do – Jump and Turn Kick
족도 돌려차기
(jok do – dohl yuh cha gi)

1. Begin in the fighting stance.

2. Slightly jump up with your left foot, shifting your body to the left.

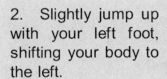

3,4. In a large horizontal circular motion, kick with the knife edge of your right foot. Try to maintain the horizontal level from beginning to the finish.

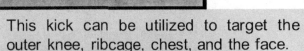

This kick can be utilized to target the outer knee, ribcage, chest, and the face.

This kick can be very lethal, so be extremely judicious when you actually execute this kick on an opponent.

Reverse Side Kick
뒤돌아 옆차기
(dwi dohl ah – yup cha gi)

1. Begin in the fighting stance.

2. From this stance shift your left hip forward by bending your knees.

3. As you bend your upper body (making it parallel to the ground) bring your right leg straight from the back position. Try to get your right heel to pass by your left ankle as close as possible.

4,5. Now execute a side kick. Make sure you pivot on your left foot. Left heel should be pointing in the direction of the kick.

Keep your body linear.

Your butt should not be sticking out in a "V" shape. Your upper back should be pulled back to assist you in keeping your body straight.

Side Kick Block
발막기
(bahl mak gi)

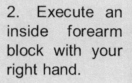

1. Begin in the fighting stance.

2. Execute an inside forearm block with your right hand.

3. Keep your kicking leg loose with hardly any power in it. Keeping loose allows you to bring your foot up very quickly.

4. Bring up your leg in a clockwise circular motion. As your leg gets up almost to your face, tilt your foot to the right with the toes pulled back so that the toes are now facing outward.

Side Kick Block

5,6.   As shown in the picture to the left, when your foot is at its highest point, the blade of your foot should be almost parallel to the ground.

From the highest point, bring your foot down with full power to block the incoming side kick as quickly as you can.

6,7. As your leg comes down your knee needs to be slightly bent in order to facilitate in executing this kick.

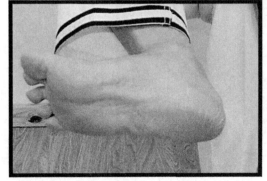

Chest Kick
족도 밀어 차 넣기
(jok do – mil uh – cha nuh ki)

1. Begin in the fighting stance.

2. Execute an inside forearm block with your right arm.

3. Bring your right thigh as close to your chest as possible by bending your knee and twisting your upper body slightly to the left.

4. As you lift up your right leg you want to position your foot vertically with the blade pointing towards your opponent. At the same time lift up on the balls of your left foot.

5,6. Extend your leg out straight in front of you. Think of this kick as a coiled spring. Coil your foot as close to the chest as possible and then release it by springing it outward forcefully, striking your opponent on the center of the chest.

Axe Kick (Heel Down Kick)
뒤꿈치 차 내리기
(dwi goom chi – cha – neh ri gi)

1. Begin in the fighting stance.

2. Execute an inside forearm block with your right hand.

3. Bring your foot up in a halfway circular motion.

4. Slightly lift up your left heel as you bring your right foot up.

Axe Kick (Heel Down Kick)

5,6.   Once you bring your foot up to the "12 o'clock" position, pull your toes back and bring it straight down as quickly as you can.

7.   As you bring down your foot you want to pull back on your upper back to counter the force you are exerting as your foot is coming down.

This kick is used to target the collar bone and the chest.

Jok Do Kick – (going up)
Stretch Kick
족도 차 올리기
(jok do – cha – ohl lee gi)

1. Begin in the fighting stance.

2. Execute an inside block with your right forearm.

3,4,5. With your toes pulled back and with the blade of your foot pointing toward your opponent, bring your leg straight up.

Again, this is a stretching kick only. Make sure and keep your knee straight and raise it up as high as you can.

Jok Do Kick – (going down)
족도 차 내리기
(jok do – cha – neh ri gi)

1. Begin in the fighting stance..

2. Execute an inside block with your right forearm.

3. With your foot loose and knees bent slightly, lift up your leg quickly.

4. You are kicking with the blade of the foot, so be sure to have the outer edge of your foot facing out.

Jok Do Kick – (going down)

5,6,7.   Lift up your leg in a semi-circle, in a clockwise direction. Once you have your leg up as high as you can, bring it down at a slight angle as fast as you can.

You are targeting your opponent's face, neck, and chest.

High Side Kick
상단 옆차기
(sahng dahn – yup cha gi)

1. Begin in the fighting stance.

This kick is done just like the regular side kick except you are now kicking higher.

2,3.   As with the side kick, begin by lifting up your leg, keeping it loose and bending at the knee. Bring it straight up above your waist height.

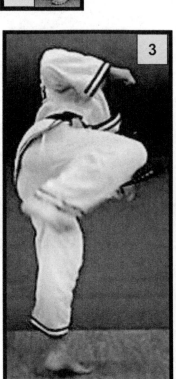

4.   As you bring your leg up, start lowering your upper body. Keeping your butt in and extending your upper back, execute the high side kick. Be sure to keep your toes pulled back and down at an angle so that you are kicking with the heel of your foot.

High Side Kick – (side profile)

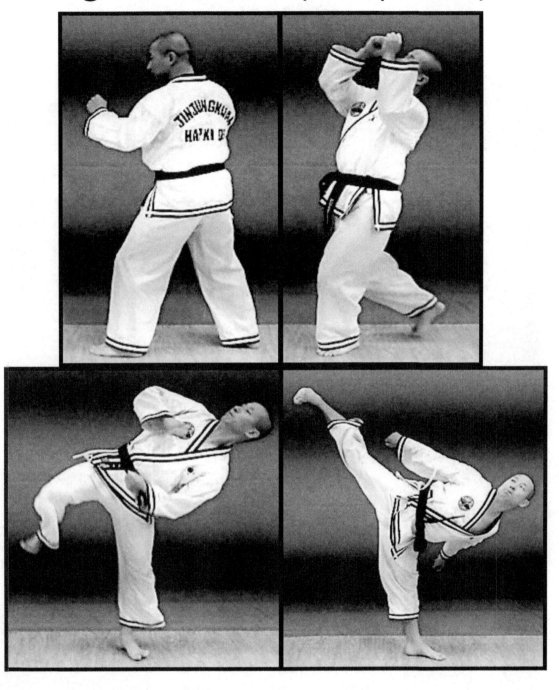

Roundhouse Kick
찍어 차기
(jjick uh – cha gi)

1. Begin in the fighting stance.

2. Keeping your leg loose, bring your knee up above your waist with the bottom half of your leg hanging loosely.

3. Now pivot on your left foot so that the heel is facing forward and the toes are pointing away from you. At the same time lower your upper body, stick in your butt and pull back on your upper back to get it straight.

4,5. Keeping your toes straight, snap your knee and kick through the target.

Remember, the power is generated at the waist as you pivot your foot and stick in your butt. All these are done simultaneously.

Roundhouse Kick – (side profile)

Heel Kick
뒤꿈치 돌여차기
(dwi goom chi – dohl yuh cha gi)

1. Begin in the fighting stance.

2,3. This kick is done with the back of your heels. Quickly lift your leg from the ground and bring it up in a circular motion.

4. Keep your knee straight and toes pulled back. Lower your body as you execute the kick. Swing the kicking leg around all the way. **Do not stop the kick at the target. KICK THROUGH the target.**

Heel Kick

This is a dangerous kick so always practice with caution. Targets for this kick are the temple, cheek/chin, ribs, and lower legs.

Notice how the kick goes all the way through bringing it almost back to the original starting position.

Back Kick
뒤 옆차기
(dwi – yup cha gi)

The back kick is utilized in situations where the opponent is approaching you from behind. The target is the opponent's kneecap or the thigh.

1. Start position.
2. Slide your left foot back to the spot where your right foot is.
3. As you move your left foot lean forward and snap your right foot straight back, fully extending the leg.
4. At this point your body should make a straight line.

This is a fast kick and you should keep facing forward while you execute the kick.

Make sure and keep your toes pulled back and strike with your heel.

Back Kick

Knee Kick
무릎 차올리기
(mu reup – cha – ohl lee gi)

1. Start position.

2. Grab the opponent's head/ shoulders with your hands.

3. Pull down in a fast motion.

4. At the same time lift up your right knee and strike your opponent on the abdomen, chest, or face. Be sure to have your toes pointing straight down.

It helps if you lean back slightly so that you can strike your opponent with your knees instead of the thighs.

Knee Kick

COMBINATION KICKS
복식족술
(bok shick jok sool)

The following set of kicks are combination kicks, or "Double Kicks". These kicks are utilized when you encounter more than one opponent or when you want to strike your opponent more than once.

The key to executing the double kicks is to start the initial kick quickly and powerfully. The speed and power from the first kick will assist you in executing the second kick. Each kick is done with full force, power, and speed. Do not think that the first kick is used as a fake kick to distract your opponent.

Inside /Outside Crescent Kick
안다리 차고 바깥다리 차기
(ahn da ri – cha goh – bak gaht da ri – cha gi)

1. Begin in the fighting stance.

2.   Execute an inside crescent kick with your right foot.

3.   Bring it down your in front of your left foot. Try to land on the balls of your foot in order to facilitate   in   executing   the upcoming outside crescent kick.

Inside /Outside Crescent Kick

4,5. Now step in with the left foot and execute an outside crescent kick. Be sure to be quick and make sure you execute the kick in a clockwise circular motion.

Jok Do Kick/Back Side Kick
족기 차고 뒤 옆차기
(jok gi – cha goh – dwi yup cha gi)

1. Begin in the fighting stance.

2. Execute a jok do kick to your opponent's right groin. Put your hip into it and lean back slightly.

3. Quickly snap the foot back and immediately execute a back side kick. This is done all in one motion so do not pause after the initial kick.

4. As you execute the back kick, bend your left knee slightly and lean your body forward for better balance and power.

Jok Do Kick / Front Side Kick
족기 지르고 앞 옆차기
(jok do – ji roo goh – ahp – yup cha gi)

1. Begin in the fighting stance.

2. Execute a jok do kick to your opponent's groin area.

3. Quickly bring your foot back. Keep your thigh at waist level and bend at the knee without putting your foot down on the ground.

4. Pivot on your left foot and execute a front side kick. Be sure to make your body linear, hips in, and upper body pulled back.

Jok Do Kick/Roundhouse Kick
족기 지르고 찍어 차기
(jok do – ji roo goh – jjick uh – cha gi)

1. Begin in the fighting stance.

2. Execute a jok do kick to the groin.

3,4. Keeping your knee up at waist level, bend your knees and immediately pivot on your left foot to execute a roundhouse kick.

Jok Do Kick/Side-Side Kick
족기 지르고 옆 옆차기
(jok gi – ji roo goh – yup – yup cha gi)

1. Begin in the fighting stance.

2. Execute a jok do kick to your opponent's right groin side.

3. Bring your foot back quickly by keeping your thigh at waist level, without touching your foot to the ground, and execute a side kick.

4. Remember, your initial kick has to be fast and powerful in order to facilitate in executing your second kick.

Low/High Side Kick
옆차기 하단 상단
(yup cha gi – ha dan – sahng dan)

1. Begin in the fighting stance.

2. Execute a low side kick to your opponent's knee area with your right foot.

3. Quickly retract the foot and complete a high side kick.

4. Be sure to lower your body to increase the height of the kick.

Inside Crescent – Front Side Kick
안다리 차고 앞 옆차기
(ahn da ri – cha goh – ahp – yup cha gi)

1,2,3.   Execute an inside crescent kick. After kicking the target, bring in your kicking foot as close to you as possible (do not put your foot down).

4.   Immediately follow up with a front side kick to your opponent.

One use for this kick: block on incoming punch with the inside crescent kick and then immediately deliver the front side kick.

Side Kick – Heel Down Kick
옆차기 뒤꿈치 차 내리기
(yup cha gi – dwi goom chi – cha neh ri gi)

1. Begin in the fighting stance.

2. Deliver a side kick to your opponent.

3. Retract the foot back halfway without touching the ground.

4. Immediately execute a heel down kick (or axe kick).

This kick is often helpful when your opponent happens to either block or grab the initial kick. If this occurs, swiftly twist free from his grab and execute the heel down kick.

Side Kick with Single Punch
한주먹 지르고 옆 옆차기
(han ju muhk – ji roo goh – yup – yup cha gi)

1. Begin in the fighting stance.

2,3. This kick is used against two opponents. If you have one in the front and the other to your side, then simultaneously deliver the punch and side kick at the same time.

Side Kick – Double Punch
양주먹 지르고 옆 옆차기
(yang ju muhk – ji roo goh – yup – yup cha gi)

1. Begin in the fighting stance.

2,3. This is the same as the previous kick except you are now targeting three opponents. Simultaneously deliver the side kick, front punch, and the side punch at the same time.

Shin Kick – Roundhouse Kick
안다리 차고 발등 찍어 차기

(ahn da ri – cha goh – bahl deung –
jjick uh – cha gi)

1. Begin in the fighting stance.

4,5. Immediately deliver a high roundhouse kick as you pivot on your base foot.

2. Deliver a shin kick to your opponent.

3. Quickly retract the foot without touching the ground.

Side Kick – Reverse Side Kick
옆차기 뒤돌아 옆차기
(yup cha gi – dwi doh ra – yup cha gi)

1. Begin in the fighting stance.

2,3.   From fighting stance, deliver a front side kick.

4.   After delivering the kick, bring the foot down in front of you.

5,6.   As soon as your kicking foot touches the ground, deliver a reverse side kick.

Jok Do Kick and Jok Do Kick
족기 차고 족기 차기
(jok gi – cha goh – jok gi – cha gi)

From a fighting stance, execute a front jok do kick with your right foot. Bring the leg back to the starting position. As soon as you bring it back, turn to your right and execute a second jok do kick with your left foot.

Jok Do Kick / Jump Roundhouse Kick
족기 차고 점프 찍어 차기
(jok gi cha go – jum poo – jjick uh cha gi)

1. 1. Begin in the fighting stance.

2

2,3. Execute a jok do kick with your left foot. Be sure to put full power into the kick.

4

4,5,6. As soon as you complete the kick, push off the ground with your right foot and execute a jump roundhouse kick.

3

5

Launch immediately into the jump roundhouse kick after the center toe kick.

6

Jok Do Kick / Jump Front Side Kick
족기 차고 점프 앞 옆차기
(jok gi cha goh – jum poo – ahp yup cha gi)

1. Begin in the fighting stance.

4. Upon completion, immediately launch into the jump front side kick.

2,3. Execute a jok do kick with your right foot.

5,6. Push off of the ground with your left foot and jump forward to execute the jump front side kick.

Jok Do Kick / Jump Side Kick

족기 차고 점프 옆 옆차기
(jok gi cha goh – jum poo – yup yup cha gi)

1

1. Begin in the fighting stance.

2

2,3. Execute a jok do kick .

3

4

Jok Do Kick / Jump Side Kick

4,5,6,7. As you bring back the kicking foot, push off of the ground with your right foot and execute a jump side kick.

Jok Do / Jump Side / Jump Side Side Kick
족기 차고 점프 옆차기 점프 옆 옆차기
(jok gi cha goh – jum poo yup cha gi – jum poo yup yup cha gi)

1. Begin in the fighting stance.

2,3,4. This is the same as the previous kick except you are adding another jump side kick.

Execute a front jok do kick to your opponent.

5,6,7. Quickly execute the 1st jump side kick.

Jok Do / Jump Side / Jump Side Side Kick

8,9,10.   As you retract your leg, quickly push off the ground and deliver the second jump side kick.

Jok Do Kick / Jump Back Kick
족기 차고 점프 뒤차기
(jok gi cha goh – jum poo – dwi cha gi)

Execute a jok do kick with your left foot. Quickly bring it back and push off of the ground to deliver the back kick. As your left foot touches the ground your right leg should be extended out to the back at a downward angle. You should be leaning forward with the body down and head up.

Side Kick / Jump Side Side Kick
옆차기 차고 점프 옆 옆차기
(yup cha gi cha goh – jum poo – yup yup cha gi)

1,2,3.   From the fighting stance, execute a side kick to the right.

Be sure to strike with your heel and make sure that your entire body is linear with your butt pushed in and your upper back pulled back.

Side Kick / Jump Side Side Kick

4,5,6,7,8. Immediately bring your leg back and execute a jump side kick to your left side.

Be sure to keep your legs loose until the moment of impact. Remember, tensing the muscles only reduces speed.

Front Side Kick / Jump Front Heel Kick
옆차기 차고 점프 뒤꿈치 돌려차기
(yup cha gi cha goh – jum poo – dwi goom chi dohl yuh cha gi)

1,2,3.   From a fighting stance, execute a front side kick with your right foot. Be sure to keep your leg loose up until the moment of impact.

4,5.   As you bring your right foot down, push forward with your back leg and use your right leg to jump up.

Front Side Kick / Jump Front Heel Kick

6,7,8. As you jump up with your right leg, bring it up in a clockwise motion to execute a jumping heel kick.

Be sure to land quickly so that you can be ready to attack or counter any possible incoming attacks.

Front Side Kick /Jump Center Knuckle Punch
옆차기 차고 점프 중지권 지르기
(yup cha gi cha goh – jum poo – joong ji gwun ji roo gi)

1,2,3,4.   From fighting stance step forward with your left foot. Bend your left knee slightly and turn your foot outward so that your toes are pointing out.

At the same time slap your thighs with your hands and quickly bring them up together into a "clap" to the left side of your face.

Immediately follow up with a front side kick with your right foot.

Front Side Kick / Jump Center Knuckle Punch

6,7,8.   As you bring down your foot push up and forward with your back leg and end with a center knuckle strike to the opponent's solar plexus.

SPECIAL KICKS
특수 발차기
(teuk soo – bahl cha gi)

Special kicks are advanced kicks which require more balance, precision, and power.

Foot work is extremely important for these kicks in order for them to be effective

The more you practice, the better your timing will be and you will develop a better sense and feel for when to best utilize these kicks.

Spinning Heel Kick
뒤돌아 뒤꿈치 돌려차기
(dwi doh ra – dwi goom chi – dohl yuh cha gi)

1.   For practice purposes, the initial stance is a sideways cat stance, with most of the weight on the back leg and partial weight on the balls of your front foot.

2.   Take a small step forward with your front foot. Use your lead foot to close the gap between you and your intended target.

3.   Next, bring your left foot around in a small clockwise circular motion. Your left foot should be about one foot away from your right foot. Lean forward, bend your knees, and angle your toes inward.

Spinning Heel Kick

5,6,7. Quickly bring your right foot up in clockwise circular motion into a heel kick. Turn your head so you can see the target.

Be sure to kick through the target instead of kicking at the target.

Bring your kicking foot all the way down to the ground back into a fighting stance for your next attack or defense.

Spinning Middle Kick
중단 돌려차기
(joong dan – dohl yuh cha gi)

1. For practice purposes, starting position is in a horse stance, knees bent slightly, left fist on your waist and right forearm across your body.

2,3. Begin by dropping your left shoulder across in a downward angle towards your right foot. At the same hop with your left foot and place it where your right foot is.

4, Simultaneously lift your right foot backwards in a clockwise motion across your body at waist height. Again, kick with your heel and kick through the target.

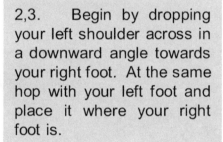

Spinning Middle Kick

5,6,7.   Once you kick through the target let the momentum of the kick bring your leg back down into a fighting stance.

With this kick you are targeting the midsection of your opponent. With practice, you should be able to execute this kick from a regular fighting stance or from a standing neutral stance.

Spinning Low Kick
앉아 하단 뒤돌아 차기
(ahn ja ha dan – dwi dohl ah cha gi)

2,3,4.   From the cat stance, take a small step forward with your lead foot.

As you do this bring your left foot around in a clockwise circular motion.

As you make the movement, drop your body to the ground.

4.   In the crouched position, your left knee should not be touching the ground. The palms of your hands are firmly on the ground, angled inward, with your head turned towards the target.

Spinning Low Kick

5,6,7. Release your right foot and execute a low heel kick in a quick circular motion. Be sure to kick through the target. Once you have kicked, use your hands to push off of the ground and back into a fighting stance.

It is important to not have your knee touching the ground. There are many practitioners who practice this kick by basically spinning on their knee to execute the kick. This is fine if you are on a soft mattress in an indoor environment; however, out on the streets (on concrete especially) you will find that you will easily tear up your knee by putting it on the ground. Also, your upper body should be bent over to facilitate executing the kick. If your upper body is not leaned forward, you will have a difficult time maintaining the required height for the kick.

Low Instep Kick
앉아 하단 발등 찍어차기
(ahn ja ha dan – bahl deung – jjick uh cha gi)

1,2.   Begin in a regular fighting stance. Take a short step forward with your lead foot, with the knees bent and the toes pointed out.

3.   Lower your body to the left, placing both palms on the ground. At the same time, extend the right leg and execute the kick.

4,5.   Use the instep of your foot to strike your target. Retract the foot and stand back up into your original fighting stance.

Intended target is the calf or the knee.

Hand Strikes
권법
(gwun bup)

Hapkido utilizes many hand strikes. There is the center knuckle, knife hand tip, hammerfist, inner hand knife, and outer knife hand strikes. The following pages will show you how to form your hand in order to properly execute the strikes.

All of the attacks are executed with power, speed, and precision. This is why it is extremely important that you not only practice the attacks on a regular basis, but you also strengthen your fingers and finger tips.

A good way of strengthening your fingertips is doing fingertip push ups. Another method is to strike your fingertips into a large bucket that has been filled with sand.

Center Knuckle
중지권
(joong ji gwun)

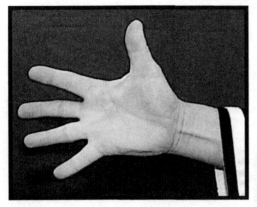

Open your hands wide.

Fold your index finger down and press your thumb down on the first phalange joint, essentially flattening the bottom half of your index finger.

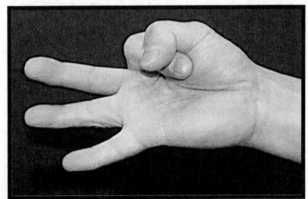

Now, curl your pinky and the fourth finger in to the palm of your hands.

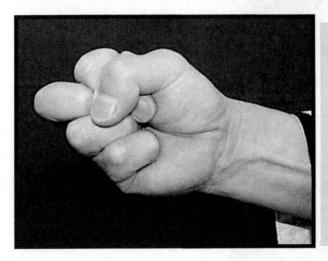

Last, curl your middle finger so that the joint of the first phalange is resting on your thumb.

This center knuckle formation allows for great strength and impact when striking your opponent on the solar plexus, throat area, or the ribcage area.

Hammerfist
망치 주먹
(mahng chi – ju muhk)

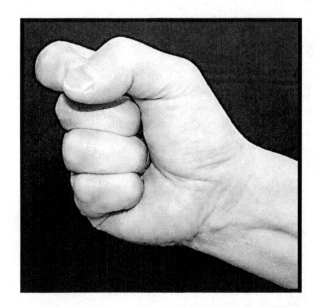

Curl the last three fingers into a fist formation, making it nice and tight.

With your index finger and the thumb, make a circle, making the fingertips touch each other. The index and thumb should not have much power into it.

You are striking an opponent with the bottom portion of the fist on the top of the head, nose, collar bone, or the chest.

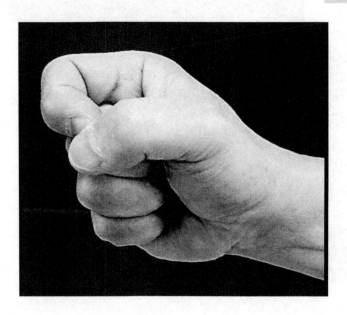

Inner Knife Hand
역수도
(yuck su do)

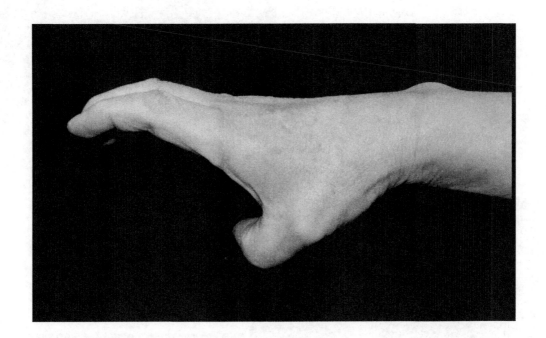

Tense your hands, curving the tips of your fingertips for added strength.   Tuck in your thumb to prevent injury to your thumb. You are striking with the inner side, the inside part next to your knuckle.

Use this to strike the temple, jaw and chest.

Center Knuckle – Solar Plexus

1. Begin in a neutral stance.

2. Step forward with your right foot. At the same time bring your left hand up to about shoulder height and form the center knuckle with your right hand.

3. As you pull in your left hand to the side of your waist, strike the opponent with your right hand center knuckle in the solar plexus.

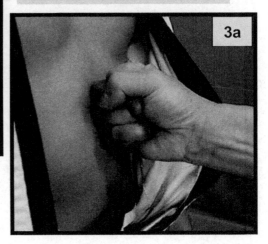

Center Knuckle - Throat

This strike is executed the same way as the previous one to the solar plexus except you are now striking to the throat (just below the adams apple).

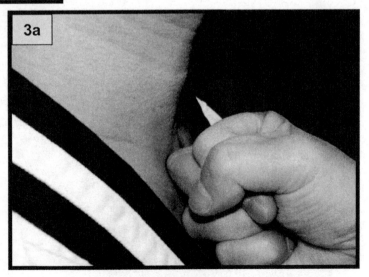

Center Knuckle – Combo Strike

1. Begin in a neutral stance.

2. Turn to your left, slide your left foot back, pull your left hand to the side of your waist and raise your right hand to shoulder height.

3. Step forward with your left foot and execute a center knuckle strike as you bring your right hand to your waist.

For steps 4 & 5, do the exact same movement done for steps 2 & 3, except in the opposite direction.

Elbow - Chin

1 Begin in neutral stance facing your opponent.

2. With your left hand, grab the top of your right hand. Bring your elbow up slightly above shoulder level. Step forward with right foot at the same time.

3,4. With the tip of your elbow strike the opponent on the chin or the jaw line, coming down at a 45 degree angle.

Be sure to drive through the target and not just stop at the chin or jaw line.

Elbow – Solar Plexus

1. Begin in neutral stance with opponent standing directly behind you.

2. As you take a step back with your right foot, pull forward your right arm.

3. In a forward/backward momentum, quickly pull back your right arm towards the opponent, striking them in the solar plexus with the point of your elbow.

Elbow – Solar Plexus / Face

1. Begin in neutral stance facing your opponent.

2. Step forward with the right foot. Move the body sideways as you swing your right arm across the front of your body.

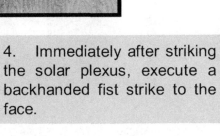

3. Next, in one quick motion, strike the solar plexus with the tip of your elbow. Be sure to strike going upwards at a 45 degree angle.

4. Immediately after striking the solar plexus, execute a backhanded fist strike to the face.

Hammerfist - Collarbone

2. Form your right hand into a hammerfist and raise it up in a circular clockwise motion as you step forward with your right foot toward your opponent.

3,4. Once your hand reaches the 2 o'clock position, bring it down quickly at a 45 degree angle on your opponent's collarbone.

Be sure to strike through the target.

Inner Hand Knife Edge - Jaw

1. Begin in neutral stance with opponent standing to your side.

2. Step in towards your opponent with the right foot. At the same time (in a scissor motion) bring right hand across your body as you bring left hand above the right arm.

3. With your right hand in the inner hand knife edge form, turn in towards the opponent and bring your right hand up towards opponent's face.

4. Strike opponent at a 45 degree angle along his jaw line.

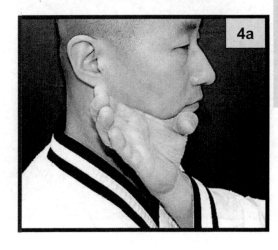

Inner Hand Knife Edge - Temple

1. Begin in neutral stance facing your opponent.

2. Raise left arm straight forward to shoulder height. Bring down right hand behind you. Step forward with left foot.

3. As you pull back your left hand back to your waist, bring your right hand up in a circular arc at a 45 degree angle to the opponent's temple.

Be sure to have your thumb tucked in underneath your palm to prevent breaking your thumb.

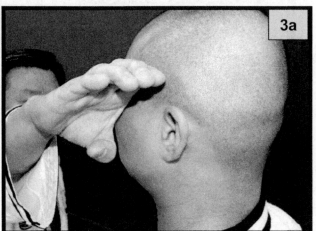

Knife Hand Blade – Neck - Temple

1. Begin in neutral stance facing your opponent.

2. Step forward with right foot. In a scissor like motion, bring the right arm across your chest and the left arm across the chest (below the right arm).

3. As you bring back your left hand to your waist, execute a neck strike with the outer blade of your hand. Be sure to strike the neck at a 45 degree angle.

4. Strike to the temple is executed exactly the same as picture #3, except you raise your arm a little higher to target the temple.

Knife Hand Tip – Solar Plexus

1. Begin in neutral stance facing your opponent.

2. Step forward with the right foot. Raise the left arm straight forward to about shoulder height. Bring the right hand (palm down) next to your waist.

3. As you pull back your left hand to your waist, thrust forward your right knife hand, striking the solar plexus with the tip of your fingers. When thrusting your right knife hand, rotate it in clockwise motion as you bring it forward.

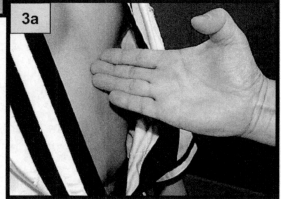

Knife Hand Tip – Throat

1. Begin in neutral stance facing your opponent.

2. Step forward with the right foot. Raise the left arm straight forward to about shoulder height. Bring the right hand (palm down) next to your waist.

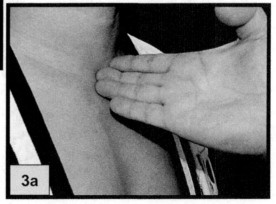

3. As you pull back your left hand to your waist, thrust forward your right knife hand, striking the throat with the tip of your fingers. When thrusting your right knife hand, rotate it in clockwise motion as you bring it forward.

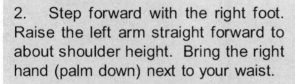

Knife Hand Tip – Neck Slice

1. Begin in neutral stance facing your opponent.

2. Slightly lift up the right foot. At the same time, raise your right arm in a clockwise oval shaped circular motion with an open knife hand and bring your left arm across your chest.

3,4. Bring your knife hand down very quickly at a 45 degree angle, slicing down your opponent's neck.

Be sure and follow through all the way down, while maintaining eye contact with your opponent.

Outer Knife Hand - Chest

1. Begin in neutral stance facing your opponent.

2. Step forward with the right foot. Bring your right arm across the front of your chest and bring the left arm across your chest, below your right arm.

3. As you pull your right arm back, strike the opponent just below his chest with the outer edge of your knife hand. Strike below the chest at a 45 degree angle.

Outer Knife Hand - Neck

1. Begin in a neutral stance with the opponent by your side.

2. Form your knife hand and raise your right arm in counter clockwise circular motion.

3. Bring your right hand across your neck in the 9 o'clock position.

4,5. Step sideways into the opponent with your right foot and execute a knife hand neck strike with the outer blade of your hand.

Outer Knife Hand – Both Sides

1. Begin in neutral stance. You have two opponents, one on your left side and one on your right side.

2. Bring up both of your arms, left arm in clockwise circular motion and the right arm in a counter clockwise circular motion.

3. As your arms come up to the 12 o'clock position, your hands are going to cross each other.

4. Then stepping to either your left or right side, continue your hand motion on through and strike both of your opponents on their neck at a 45 degree angle with the outer edge of your knife hand.

Backhand Fist - Temple

1. Begin in a neutral stance facing the opponent.

2.   Step forward with the right foot. Bring your right arm across the front of your chest and bring the left arm across your chest, below your right arm.

3.   As you pull your left hand to your waist, make a backhanded fist and strike the opponent on the temple with your first two knuckles.

3 Strike Combo

In this combination strike, you are imagining that you are facing three opponents. One in front, one on the side, and one to the back.

Step forward with your right foot and execute a center knuckle strike to the solar plexus of the opponent directly in front of you.

Next, swing your back leg around 90 degrees in a counter clockwise motion and execute a outer hand knife to the neck or temple of the opponent standing to the side.

Finally, step forward with your right foot and execute a center knuckle strike to the solar plexus or throat of the opponent that was standing directly behind you. By the time you are ready to execute this strike, you should be facing this opponent.

Self-Defense Techniques

Hapkido techniques are designed to effectively immobilize an opponent by the use of pressure points and joint locks. The purpose of Hapkido is not to permanently injure and destroy an opponent, rather, it is to use just enough force to neutralize the attack and render the opponent impotent. This is why Hapkido is considered a "gentleman's" martial art.

Any strong thug can punch a weaker man into a pulp, but only a true gentleman with strength, discipline, and confidence can remain calm and exercise restraint when confronted with a threatening situation.

It cannot be emphasized enough that **Practice Makes Perfect**. Practice, practice, and practice some more in order to master the skills and keep them razor sharp. If you happen to be one of those individuals who thinks that merely knowing the techniques will be sufficient to defend against an attack, you are sadly mistaken. Mastery of any skill does not come overnight, nor does it occur after a week's worth of training. You must practice a technique hundreds of times so that it becomes second nature. Anyone who has ever been in a fight will tell you that there is no time to consider which technique will be the best to use in that particular situation. The situation as a whole is assessed immediately and reacted upon just as quickly. In order to get to that level, you simply must practice every single day.

In Hapkido, we have what is called "LIVE HAND". This means that the moment someone grabs your wrist, you open your hand wide and put power into it. If you hold your right wrist with your left hand and squeeze hard, you will be able to tell the difference between keeping your hands closed versus keeping them open.

Self-Defense Techniques

While the pictures here depict only the wrist grabs to the right side, you should make it a habit to practice from both hands for ambidexterity. Remember to always maintain eye contact with your opponent when executing any of the techniques. As you progress and develop, you will soon be able to see/predict your opponent's next actions.

The techniques themselves should be completed in one fluid motion. Speed is not essential when you are first starting out. Practice on perfecting the form and being able to do them without jerky, separate motions. Only after mastering the form should you consider increasing the speed.

Remember that every aspect of each technique is important. You must first safely defend against an attack so that you can transition for the offensive attack. Furthermore, your attack must be quick accurate, and powerful in order for it to be effective.

Basic Wrist Escapes

기번 손목빼기

(gi buhn – sohn mohk ppeh gi)

Basic Wrist Escape – (1)

1. At the moment of grab, make your hands "LIVE".

2. Keeping a "LIVE" hand, step forward with your right foot as you twist your wrist in a counter clockwise motion.

3. Continue moving forward as you twist your wrist counter clockwise. Maintain eye contact with your opponent. Free your wrist from his grasp.

Be sure to keep your right arm straight and stiff. Do not bend your elbow.

This is an exercise in learning wrist escape. Keep your arm and fingers fully tensed and always maintain eye contact with your opponent.

Basic Wrist Escape – (2)

1. At the moment of grab, make your hands "LIVE".

2. Keeping a "LIVE" hand, step forward with your right foot. At the same time bend your elbow and raise your hand to your chest level, keeping your forearm parallel to the ground.

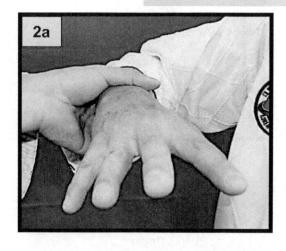

3. While continuing the forward momentum, drive forward and pretend you are delivering an elbow strike to the opponent's chest. Your wrist should be released from the opponent's grasp.

Maintain eye contact with your opponent.

Basic Wrist Escape – (3)

1. At the moment of grab, make your hands "LIVE".

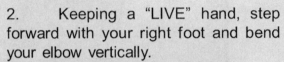

2. Keeping a "LIVE" hand, step forward with your right foot and bend your elbow vertically.

3,4. Maintaining eye contact, continue to drive forward as if you were delivering an upper elbow strike to the opponent's face.

Basic Wrist Escape – (4)

1. The opponent grabs your wrist and is pulling you towards him.

2. Keeping a "LIVE" hand pull back against the opponent's pull just for a split second.

3. Quickly burst in with a small step. As you do so, slip your hand under and out to the outside of his wrist.

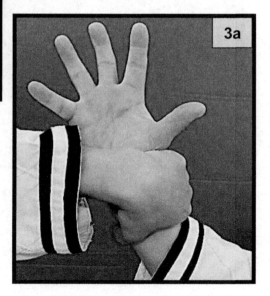

Basic Wrist Escape – (5)

1. At the moment of grab, make your hands "LIVE".

2. Keeping a "LIVE" hand, bend your knees slightly as you step back with your right foot.

3. Continue the backward momentum as you bend your elbow and bring your hand to the outside of his wrist.

4. Keeping your forearm, wrist, and hands vertical, straighten the legs. Your opponent should be leaning forward against your pull.

Basic Wrist Escape – (6)

1. At the moment of grab, make your hands "LIVE".

2. Bend your knees slightly and push down with your right arm, making sure to keep your arm straight.

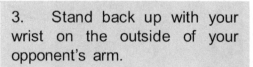

2a. Bring your hand up and to the outside of his wrist.

3. Stand back up with your wrist on the outside of your opponent's arm.

Basic Wrist Escape – (7)

1. At the moment of grab, make your hand "LIVE".

2. Step diagonally with your left foot and bring your hand under and out, to the outside of his wrist, keeping your bicep close to your ribcage.

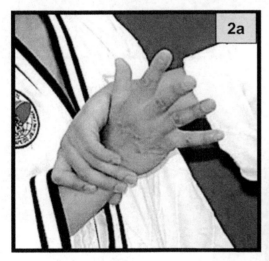

3. Step back (counter clockwise) with your right foot and bring your right hand towards your chest, pulling in your opponent.

Basic Wrist Escape – (8)

1. At the moment of grab, make your hand "LIVE".

2. Step diagonally to the right.

3. At the same time bring your hand to the outside of his wrist.

4. Slide your left foot behind your right and bend your right elbow to finish the move.

Joint Lock Techniques
호신술 (ho shin sool)

Same Side Wrist Grab
같은 쪽에서 한손목 잡였을 때
(gaht eun jjohk eh suh han sohn mohk jahp yuht seul tteh)

Same Side Wrist Grab (1)

1. At the moment of grab, make your hand "LIVE".

2. Bend your right elbow and lift your right hand straight up. Your right palm should be facing you and be at about shoulder level.

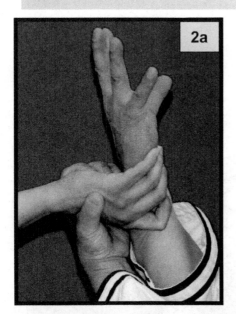

3. Bring your left hand under your opponent's and wrap your fingers firmly around the thumb pad to get a good grasp on the back of his hand.

Same Side Wrist Grab (1)

4.   Free the right hand from his grasp and place your right palm on the back of your opponent's hand. Your left thumb and your right thumb should be right next to each other.

5.   Step forward with your right foot and apply pressure on the opponent's wrist by twisting it in a clockwise motion. Your opponent's elbow and wrist should be at a 45 degree angle for maximum effect.

6.   Maintain eye contact with your opponent.

If you see that your opponent is about to strike you with his free hand, then immediately step back with your right foot and pull his arm down to the ground.

Same Side Wrist Grab (2)

1. At the moment of grab, make your hand "LIVE".

2.　　Slightly bend your right elbow, step forward with your right foot, and push against your opponent's hand with your forearm. Your forearm should be at an upward 45 degree angle.

3.　　As you slide your right foot back swing your right hand down and up clockwise.

Same Side Wrist Grab (2)

4. At the same time use your left hand to grab your opponent's left hand. Your left thumb should be faced downward, grasping the back of the opponent's hand near their thumb and the rest of your fingers should be grabbing the meaty part of their palms.

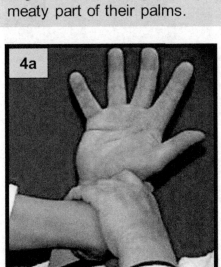

5,6,7. Bring your right elbow forward and up, breaking your opponent's thumb / step in with the right foot (going diagonally to the left) / and execute a **Kalnukki** to the pressure point just above his elbow. Make sure you execute this with the knife edge of your forearm and not your wrist.

Same Side Wrist Grab (2)

Be sure to follow along with the picture carefully. Notice how Grandmaster Kim is grabbing the opponent's hand and his body position in relation to the opponent.

The elbow pressure point is three finger spaces up from the elbow.

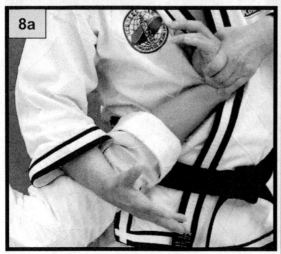

Same Side Wrist Grab (3)

1. At the moment of grab, make your hand "LIVE".

2. Grab the opponent's wrist as you step in with the left leg. Continue turning your body so that the entire length of your arm is straight. This extracts your wrist as well as sets you up for the attack.

Move your arm and body at a slight angle, making your right arm and the opponent's left arm almost parallel to each other.

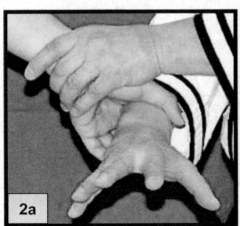

Same Side Wrist Grab (3)

4,5.   Keeping his hand close to your chest, step in and execute a **Kalnukki** to his arm just above the elbow.

Once more, the ideal place to strike would be 3 finger spaces above the opponent's elbow. This is the perfect spot to hyperextend the arm.

Be sure and not to bend your body down as you execute the knife hand strike, thereby relieving the pressure being applied. Instead, keep more of an upright position and use a see-saw motion of your upper body to execute the move.

Same Side Wrist Grab (4)

1. At the moment of grab make your hand "LIVE".

2. Step in with your left foot, with toes pointed out and knees slightly bent.

3. Keeping the right arm straight, grab his left wrist with your left hand and turn your body so that your arm and his arm are parallel to each other.

4. Release your right wrist from the opponent's grasp and execute a right elbow strike to your opponent's chest as you pull on their left arm with your left hand.

Same Side Wrist Grab (4)

5. Grab the opponent's left hand with both of your hands and execute a side kick as you duck under his arm.

6,7,8. As you put your right foot down execute a wrist joint lock (same side wrist grab -1) as you bring your left foot back.

In picture #5, if you do not have a second opponent you do not execute the side kick, instead, you just go under his arm.

Same Side Wrist Grab (5)

1. At the moment of grab, make your hands "LIVE".

2.   Bring your right hand up to shoulder level as you grasp the opponent's wrist between your thumb and index finger. Your left hand should cover the back of his hand as well.

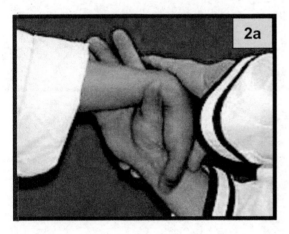

3. Step forward with your right foot, bringing your left hand close to your chest. Make sure you hold your opponent's hand tight to your chest. Bring your right elbow up and over the opponent's arm at the bend of the elbow.

Same Side Wrist Grab (5)

4. Use your elbow to bend his arm. Keeping a firm grip of his hand, press down on his arm.

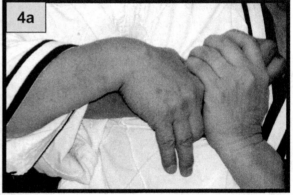

5. Continue the downward pressure on the opponent's arm. Maintain eye contact at all times.

The key point here is to keep applying pressure on his wrist and to maintain the wrist out at a 45 degree angle.

Same Side Wrist Grab (6)

1. At the moment of grab, make your hand "LIVE".

2. Step forward diagonally towards the opponent. At the same time, twist your "LIVE" hand palm up and push it towards him as you pull at his elbow.

3. Continue the forward momentum and wrap the left hand around their elbow. Be sure to keep their arm close to your body.

Same Side Wrist Grab (6)

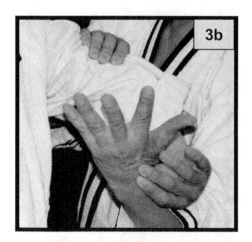

Notice how Grandmaster Kim allows very little space between himself and the opponent. This permits easier control of the opponent. If there is too much space, the opponent can easily free himself by straightening out his arm.

4a, 4b.   With the firm grip on his arm you can either pull back on his shoulder, neck, or the head to maintain maximum control.

Same Side Wrist Grab (7)

1. At the moment of grab, make your hand "LIVE".

2, 3.   Bring your "LIVE" hand up and to the outside of the opponent's wrist.   As you do so, place your left hand on the back of his hand to keep it firmly secure.

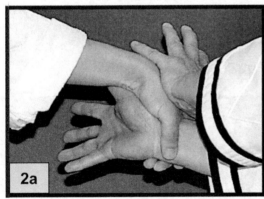

Same Side Wrist Grab (7)

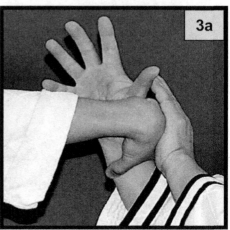

4,5. When your right hand is up to your shoulder level, drive it down at a 45 degree angle as you step in with your right foot.

The key point here is to lock their wrist at the 45 degree angle position. This position provides for maximum efficacy.

Same Side Wrist Grab (8)

1. At the moment of grab, make your hand "LIVE".

2. Step forward diagonally as you free your arm from the opponent's grasp.

3. Continuing with the forward momentum, use both hands to grab his right hand.

4. Lift up his arm to shoulder level and step under it.

Same Side Wrist Grab (8)

5. Go under the opponent's right arm.

6. Turn your body counter-clockwise while twisting the opponent's right wrist.

How to grab your opponent's hand:
Your thumbs are on the back of the opponent's hand. Your middle, fourth, and pinky fingers are grabbing the meaty part of the opponent's palm. You are twisting it counter-clockwise and pulling it down at a 45 degree angle.

This is not a gradual pulling and twisting of the wrist. It is done quickly and forcefully.

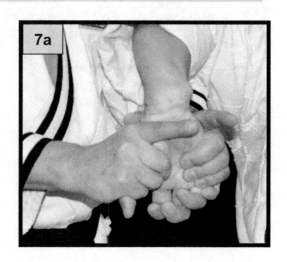

Joint Lock Techniques
호신술

Cross Hand Wrist Grab
반대 손목 (역수) 잡였을 때
(bahn deh sohn mohk (yuck su) jahp yuht seul tteh)

Cross Hand Grab (1)

1. At the moment of grab, make your hand "LIVE".

2. With your left hand grab your opponent's right hand. Your left thumb will be on the back of the opponent's hand with the rest of your fingers grabbing his palm.

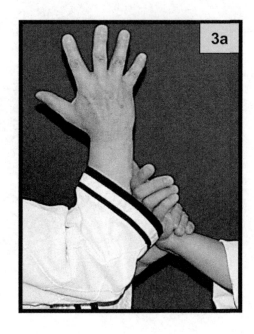

3. Step diagonally to the left with your right foot and extract your "LIVE" hand.

Cross Hand Grab (1)

4. As soon as you are free from his grasp, roll your wrist to apply pressure against his wrist. You are using the blade of your forearm to press against the back of his hand.

5. Be sure to get your opponent's wrist and elbow at a 45 degree angle for maximum effect.

As always, maintain eye contact.

Cross Hand Grab (2)

1. At the moment of grab, make your hand "LIVE".

2. Step with your right foot, going diagonally to the right. At the same time, bend your elbow and bring your wrist up to shoulder height.

3. Extend your right arm as you grab the opponent's wrist.

4,5. Step forward with the left foot and execute a **Kalnukki** to his arm just above the elbow. Reference (same side wrist grab – 2) for Kalnukki.

Remember, the ideal point of contact should be three finger spaces above the elbow.

Cross Hand Grab (3)

1. At the moment of grab, make your hand "LIVE".

2. Step forward diagonally to the left and grab the opponent's right hand with your left hand. As you do this, twist your right wrist, palm down, to release his hold.

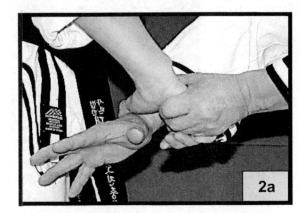

2a. Ideally, you want to grab the edge of his palm with your thumb securely pressed on the back of his hand.

3. Using both hands to grab his, step in with the right leg.

Cross Hand Grab (3)

4. Go under your opponent's arm and quickly do a 180 degree turn by pivoting on the balls of your feet.

5. Twist the opponent's hand at a 45 degree angle, in a downward motion.

If you do this hard and fast enough, you will either break his wrist or your opponent will be forced to flip over if he wants his wrist to remain intact.

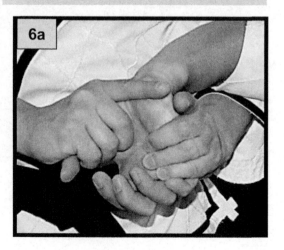

Cross Hand Grab (4)

1. At the moment of grab, make your hand "LIVE".

2. As you step forward with your left foot raise the opponent's hand by applying pressure on his wrist using your thumb and index finger. Your other 3 fingers are grabbing the back of his hand.

3,4. Quickly yank the hand back down. This quick motion is used to enter into the next move as well as to surprise your opponent and disorient him.

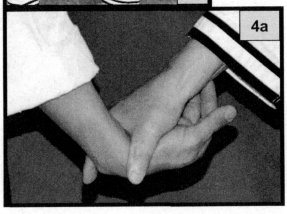

Cross Hand Grab (4)

5. Immediately follow up by swinging your right foot back clockwise and lifting your right hand over your head.

6,7. As you complete a 180 degree turn begin pulling his arm down to the ground.

8. Press your knee against his bent arm for complete control.

Cross Hand Grab (4)
(view from another angle)

Cross Hand Grab (4)
(view from another angle)

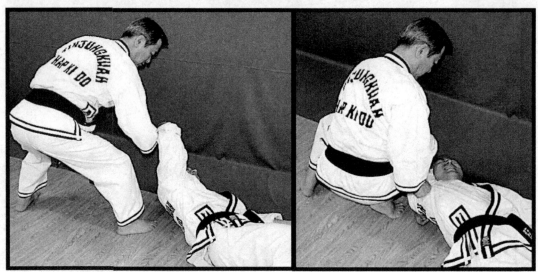

Cross Hand Grab (5)

1. At the moment of grab, make your hand "LIVE".

2. Initial step is the same as the previous technique. Lift his hand up and yank it down quickly.

Cross Hand Grab (5)

5,6. Swing your right foot around the back in clockwise motion and insert your left arm (bent at the elbow) as deep as you can just above your opponent's elbow.

7. Now as you push down with your right hand pull up at an angle with your left hand. Be sure to keep your left hand live. **The aim here is to hyperextend his arm by using your left forearm as the support for the hyperextension.**

Cross Hand Grab (6)

1. At the moment of grab make your hand "LIVE".

2. Step forward with your right foot as you bring his hand up to shoulder level. At the same time, bring your left palm up and press it against the opponent's hand.

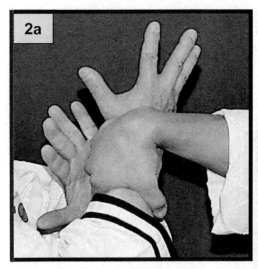

3. Twist your right wrist so that your palm is facing down and firmly press it against his wrist.

Cross Hand Grab (6)

4. Drive forward and downward at a 45 degree angle.

Make sure to keep your left hand pressed against his hand for control.

This movement should be executed with speed, accuracy, and power. All movements must be decisive and quick.

Strikes
치기 (chi gi)

Same Side Wrist Grab
같은 편에서 손목 잡였을 때

Shirt Grab From Behind-Neck
뒤에서 한손으로 목덜미 잡혔을 때

Strikes - Same Side Wrist Grab (1)

1. At the moment of grab, make your hand "LIVE".

2,3. Step forward with your right foot and extract your hand from his grasp.

4. As soon as you are free, follow up immediately with an elbow strike to the solar plexus. This should be done at an upward angle.

5. After the elbow strike, continue the attack with a backhand fist to the face.

Strikes – Same Side Wrist Grab (2)

1. At the moment of grab, make your hand "LIVE".

2,2a. Bend your right wrist inward, with fingers tensed and wide.

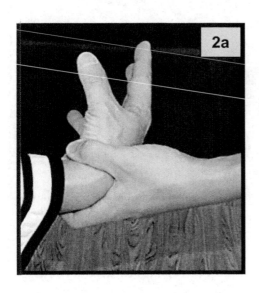

3. With a closed fist, raise your left arm high above your head.

Strikes – Same Side Wrist Grab (2)

4, 4a.   Immediately bring down your arm and strike the opponent on the inner wrist pressure point (which is three finger width up from the wrist bone) with your outer wrist bone.

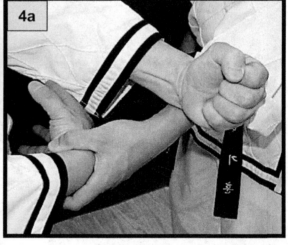

5.   After the initial strike, bring your left arm up and initiate a knife hand strike to the neck.

Strikes – Same Side Wrist Grab (2)

6. Bring your hand back close to your ear.

7,8. Deliver a knife hand strike to the neck.

To form the knife hand, straighten the hand with fingers pressed together, the thumb bent and apart from the index finger.

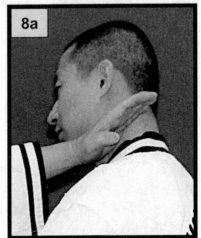

Strikes – Same Side Wrist Grab (3)

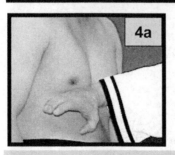

1. At the moment of grab, make your hand "LIVE".

2. Step forward and extract your hand from his grasp.

4. With your knees slightly bent, form the knife hand.

4,4a. Immediately strike him just underneath his breast, using the edge of your knife hand and strike at a 45 degree angle.

Strikes – Same Side Wrist Grab (3)

5. While maintaining eye contact, retract your arm and follow up with a strike to the side of the neck.

6. Your hand should be slanted in a 45 degree angle, striking just below the jaw.

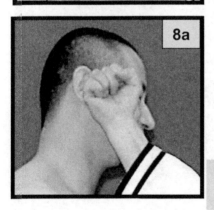

8. Swiftly execute a backhanded strike to the temple. All of these strikes should be executed in quick succession, one right after the other.

Strikes – Same Side Wrist Grab (4)

1. At the moment of grab, make your hand "LIVE".

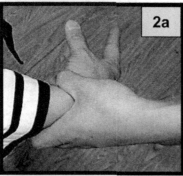

2, 2a. Keeping your fingers spread, bend at the wrist so that your palm Is now facing your body.

3,4.   Step forward with your left foot (stepping in towards the opponent's left foot). At the same time lift up your left hand in a closed fist and quickly bring it down to strike his wrist.

Remember to strike using the outer edge of your wrist bone.

Strikes – Same Side Wrist Grab (4)

5.   As soon as you strike the opponent on the wrist, release your right hand from his grasp and turn clockwise for an elbow strike.

6,7. Deliver an elbow strike to the solar plexus, striking up at a 45 degree angle.

8.   Immediately follow up with a back hand strike to the face.

Strikes – Same Side Wrist Grab (5)

1. At the moment of grab, make your hand "LIVE".

2. Step forward diagonally to your right as you raise your arm to your shoulder level.

3. Continue forward movement diagonally. Bring your left foot in front of your right foot, and go under the opponent's arm.

4,5. As you go under, turn your body towards your opponent.

Keeping your left leg bent, deliver a heel kick to your opponent's solar plexus, chest, throat, or face.

Strikes – Same Side Wrist Grab (5)
(view from another angle)

Shirt Grab - Behind – Neck (1)

1. Opponent grabs the back of your shirt from behind.

2. Bend your knees to lower your body as you rotate your body to the right.

3. Execute a knife hand strike to the ribcage.

Shirt Grab – Behind – Neck (1)

4, 5.   Quickly rotate in the other direction and execute a knife hand strike to the side of the neck.

You want to strike the opponent's neck from the open (live) side. It would be difficult to attempt a neck strike on the side of the raised arm.

Joint Lock Techniques:
호신술 (ho shin sool)
Wrist Grab From the Side
옆에서 손목 잡혔을 때
(yup peh suh sohn mohk jahp peuht seul tteh)

Wrist Grab – Side (1)

1. At the moment of grab, make your hand "LIVE".

2. Grab his hand with your left hand.

Your left thumb is placed on the back of his hand and the rest of your fingers are grasping the inside part of his palm.

Lift up your right hand slightly by bending your elbow.

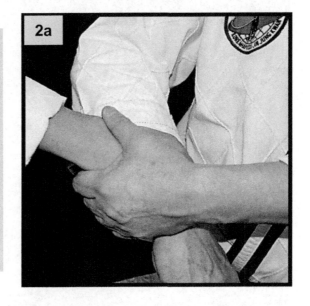

Wrist Grab – Side (1)

3. Grab the opponent by the thumb pad and lift your elbow and place it on top his forearm.

4. Step to the right side slightly and lean your entire upper body to the right side to apply pressure on the wrist joint.

Wrist Grab – Side (2)

1. At the moment of grab, make your hand "LIVE".

2,3.   Bring your right hand up to face level, and grab his wrist with your left hand.

4.   Keeping your hand "LIVE", pull his arm towards your chest as you lift your elbow up and over his forearm.

Wrist Grab – Side (2)

5.   While you keep a firm grip on his wrist, press down on his hand with the edge of your forearm.

Wrist Grab – Side (2)

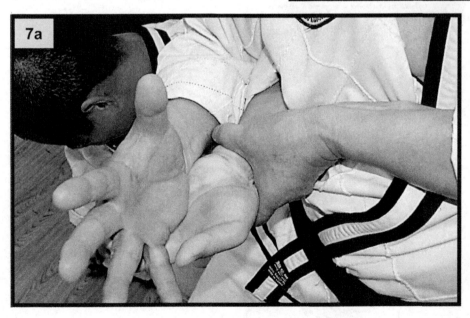

Wrist Grab – Side (3)

1. At the moment of grab, make your hand "LIVE".

2,3.   Step forward diagonally with your right foot. Grab his hand and release yours from his hold at the same time.

Wrist Grab – Side (3)

4. Immediately place your hands on top of each other so that your upper arm is slightly positioned above the opponent's elbow.

5,6. Take another step forward with your right foot and apply pressure against his arm. By using speed and proper form, you should easily hyperextend the elbow.

Warning!
Be extra careful when practicing this technique. There is a strong chance you can injure your partner if you are not fully paying attention to what you are doing. Always concentrate when training!

Joint Lock and Strike Techniques:
호신술 / 치기
Wrist Grab Both Hands
두 손으로 두 손목을 잡혔을 때
(doo sohn euh roh doo sohn mohk eul jahp peuht seul tteh)

Both Wrist Grab – Break (1)

1. Opponent grabs both of your wrists.

2. Step forward with your right foot. At the same time bring your right palm to your chest and place your left palm on your opponent's hand.

3. Bring your right elbow up and over your opponent's forearm.

Both Wrist Grab – Break (1)

4.   Now bend his arm at the elbow and lean towards him by bending at the waist.

5.   It is important to not lower your entire body as you execute this technique; just bend your knees slightly and tilt your upper body to the side at a 45 degree angle. Again, execute this technique in one quick motion.

Both Wrist Grab – Break (2)

1. Opponent grabs both of your wrists.

2. Immediately make your hands "LIVE". Bring your left palm up to face level as you grab the back of his hand with your right.

This is the same execution as the technique done for Same Side Wrist Grab #1.

3. Extricate your wrist from his grasp.

193

Both Wrist Grab – Break (2)

4.   Grab his hand (above the knuckles) with your left.

5.   Step forward with your left foot and execute the wrist lock at a 45 degree angle. Maintain eye contact with your opponent.

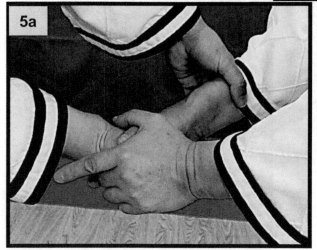

This technique can be done to either of the opponent's hand.

Both Wrist Grab – Break (3)

1. Opponent grabs both of your wrists.

2.   Make your hand "LIVE" and dip your arms straight down.

3.   Immediately pull the hands up to your shoulder level, with palms facing upward, grabbing the inside of the opponent's wrists.

Both Wrist Grab – Break (3)

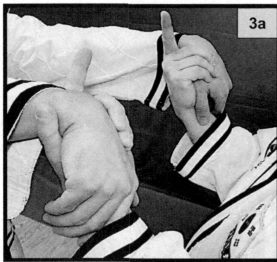

3a.   Try to keep your index fingers straight. This allows for more power, thus more pressure on the opponent's wrists.

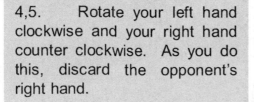

4,5.   Rotate your left hand clockwise and your right hand counter clockwise. As you do this, discard the opponent's right hand.

Both Wrist Grab – Break (2)

6. Continue to rotate your left wrist in a clockwise motion so that his elbow is facing the sky.

7,8. Step back with your right leg as you execute a reverse **Kalnukki**.

Both Wrist Grab – Break (3)

1. Opponent grabs both of your wrists.

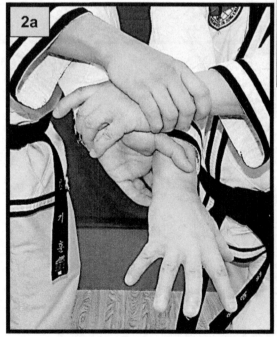

2,2a.   Step diagonally to the left. Simultaneously bring your right arm (kept straight) diagonally at a 45 degree angle. Your right arm and the opponent's left arm should almost be parallel. At the same time, grab his left wrist with your left hand.

Both Wrist Grab – Break (3)

3,4.   Extract your right wrist and bring it around to firmly cup your left hand.

Now, step forward with your right foot and push on his elbow using the upper part of your arm. This is just another way to hyperextend an opponent's arm.

Take caution when practicing this technique with a partner. In order to avoid any injuries, practice executing this technique in a slow continuous motion. As you develop your Hapkido skills and power control, you can practice with more speed and power.

Both Wrist Grab – Break (4)

1. Opponent grabs both of your wrists.

2,2a.   Step forward with your right foot. Bend your left arm so that your palm is facing down and your forearm is parallel to the ground, and press it against his fingers as you pull on the right wrist with your right hand.

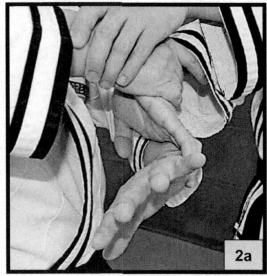

Both Wrist Grab – Break (4)

3,4.　Maintain your hold on his wrist and step under his arm. This effectively results in a wrist lock.　From this position, you can take him to the ground for added control.

Both Wrist Grab – Break (5)

1. Opponent grabs both of your wrists.

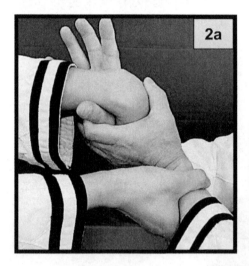

2,2a. Raise your right hand to your shoulder level. As you do this, cup the opponent's left wrist between your thumb and index finger. With your left hand, firmly support it against the back of his hand.

3. Quickly execute a side kick against the opponent.

Both Wrist Grab — Break (5)

4,4a. Just as quickly, resume a horse stance and pull up on his hand as you push down on his wrist.

Execute this pull / push motion with speed and power. This is another variation of a wrist lock.

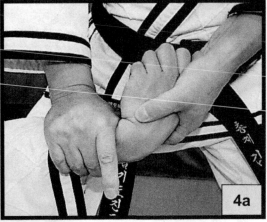

5. Take your opponent to the ground for complete control.

Both Wrist Grab – Break (6)

1. Opponent grabs both of your wrists.

2. Step in diagonally to your left, grabbing his wrist and keeping your right arm straight.

Be sure to bend your left knee, with your toes pointing out.

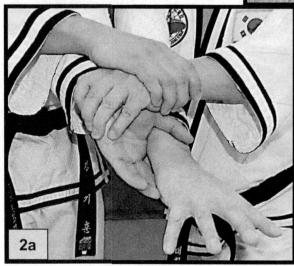

2a. Your right arm should be almost parallel with your opponent's left arm.

Both Wrist Grab – Break (6)

3.
Maintaining your grip on his wrist, step under his arm.

4. As soon as you step through, push off of your right leg and hyperextend his arm, using the upper part of your left arm. Be sure to place your upper arm firmly against the spot just above his elbow for optimal effect.

Both Wrist Grab – Break (6)

6,7.   After the initial elbow break, pull back on the wrist and push it straight towards him, twisting the wrist as you do so.

Both Wrist Grab – Strikes (1)

1. Opponent grabs both of your wrists.

2. Immediately open your hands and dip them downward. This is done to divert the opponent's energy to facilitate the execution of the technique. This immediately displaces the energy which will allow you to use it against him.

3. Raise your hands up together with the opponent's. His wrists should be placed at the curve of your hands.

Both Wrist Grab – Strikes (1)

4. Bring your hands together quickly, thereby causing the backs of his wrists to strike together.

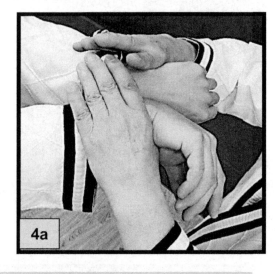

5,6. Immediately take a slight step back and execute a side kick.

Both Wrist Grab – Strikes (2)

Opponent grabs both of your wrists.

2.   Step slightly diagonally forward to the left with your left foot. At the same time, keeping your right arm straight and palms parallel to the ground, bring your arm straight back. With your right arm, cup his right wrist between your thumb and index finger and raise it up in a clockwise circular motion towards his head.

3. The above steps are executed simultaneously. Now, at the same time, strike your opponent on his left ribcage with your right knee. Be sure to keep your toes pointed down and strike with your knee, not your thigh.

Both Wrist Grab – Strikes (3)

1. Opponent grabs both of your wrists.

2, 3.   Keeping a "LIVE" hand, take a slight step forward with your left foot. At the same time, while keeping your fingers wide open and palms facing the ground, pull both arms back in a circular motion. As you do this, execute a knee kick to the chest.

Be sure to keep your toes pointed down and strike with your knee, not your thigh.

Wrist Grab from Behind (1)

1. Opponent grabs both of your wrists from behind.

2. Make your hands "LIVE". Bend your knees, lean slightly forward, and slide your right foot back.

3. Bring both of your arms up at a 45 degree angle, angling your hands inward as it gets to your face level.

As you angle your hands inward, grab your opponent's left hand with your right. Your right thumb is firmly planted on the back of his hand and the rest of your fingers are firmly grasping the meaty part of his palm.

Wrist Grab from Behind (1)

5

5,6.　　Bring his hand up and over to your right. Step to the right as you do this so that it is executed in one motion.

6

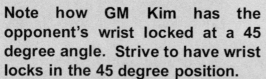

Note how GM Kim has the opponent's wrist locked at a 45 degree angle. Strive to have wrist locks in the 45 degree position.

7

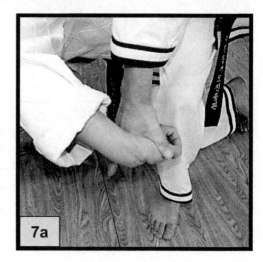

7a

Wrist Grab from Behind (2)

1. Opponent grabs both of your wrists from behind.

2. Keeping a "LIVE" hand, pivot on the ball of your left foot to turn to your right. At the same time, grab your opponent's left wrist with your left hand and grab his right wrist with your right hand. All this should be executed in one motion.

3,4. Place your right foot behind his legs. With your right hand, pull his arm up and over the head as you pull on his left arm. Placing your leg behind his leg prevents him from stepping backward, thus enabling you to make him fall backwards.

Wrist Grab from Behind (3)

1. Opponent grabs both of your wrists from behind.

This is executed exactly like the previous technique except this time you are bringing his right arm straight across his face.

Wrist Grab from Behind (4)

1. Opponent grabs both of your wrists from behind keeping your hands close together.

2. Immediately make both hands "LIVE". Slide your left hand up as you slide your right hand down.

3. Pivot on the ball of your left foot to turn to your right. As you do so, grab his left wrist with your right hand. Keep your left palm facing out.

Wrist Grab from Behind (4)

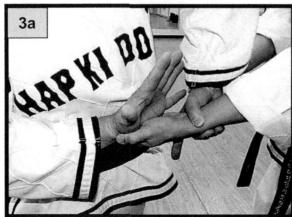

4,5.   Take a step back diagonally with your right foot and execute a basic wrist lock. (reference "same side wrist grab -1").

Wrist Grab from Behind (5)

1 Opponent grabs both of your wrists from behind keeping your hands close together.

2

2.   Pivot on the balls of your feet to turn right. Keeping your left hand open, use your right elbow to strike down on the opponent's wrist.

2a

Wrist Grab from Behind (5)

3,4.   Immediately step back diagonally with the right foot and firmly grab his wrist.

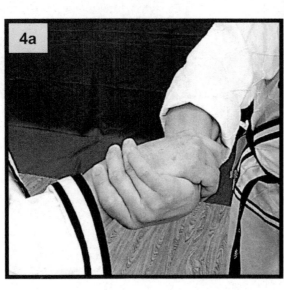

Wrist Grab from Behind (5)

5,6.   Step forward with the left leg and execute a swift **Kalnukki** to his arm just above the elbow.

For **Kalnukki** reference "same side wrist grab -2".

Joint Lock Techniques:
호신술
Sleeve Grabs
소매 잡혔을 때
(soh meh jahp peuht seul tteh)

Low Sleeve Grab (1)

1. At the moment of grab make your hands "LIVE".

2.   Bring your right hand up to eye level, with the palm facing you. At the same time grab the back of his hand with your left.

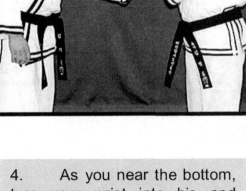

3.   Keeping a firm grip on his hand, turn your right palm vertically and bring it straight down.

4.   As you near the bottom, turn your wrist into his and bring it up sharply. When done in one motion it should look like you are forming the letter "J".

Low Sleeve Grab (1)

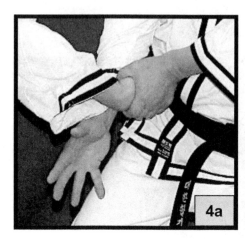

4a

Speed is essential for this technique. The power to inflict pain comes from the fast upward thrust motion.

5

5a

Low Sleeve Grab (2)

1. At the moment of grab make your hand "LIVE".

2. Grab the opponent's hand with your thumb pressed against his thumb pad.

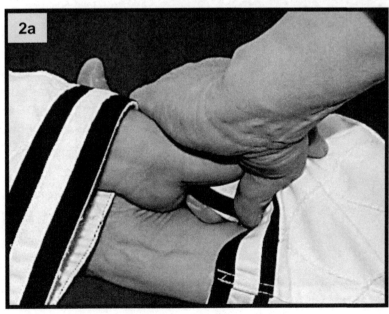

Low Sleeve Grab (2)

3. Step straight forward with your right foot. At same time bring your right hand up and over the top of the opponent's wrist.

4. Bring your right hand down in a scooping motion all the while applying pressure on the wrist with your left hand.

Mid Sleeve Grab

1. Opponent grabs you on the middle part of your shirt sleeve.

2,3. Firmly press the back of his hand with your left.

At the same time, lift up your right hand so that you trap the opponent's hand between your forearm and bicep.

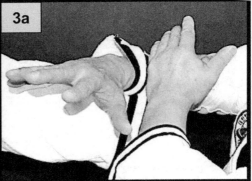

Mid Sleeve Grab

4.	Bring your right elbow down in a "U" shape. Have your elbow very close to your body.

5.	Tilt your shoulder down as you bring your palm across the front of your body, essentially locking his wrist in the 45 degree position.

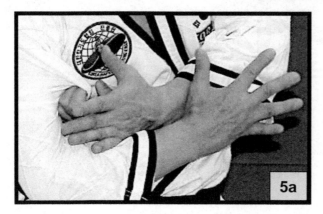

Upper Sleeve Grab (1)

1. Opponent grabs the upper part of your shirt sleeve.

2. With your left hand firmly press it against the opponent's hand.

3. Next, raise your right elbow up so that the palm of your right hand is on the right side of your chest.

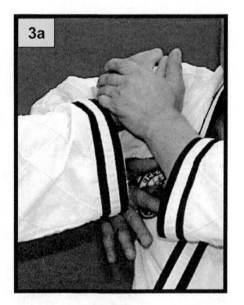

Upper Sleeve Grab (1)

4. Step forward diagonally and lean your shoulder at a 45 degree angle.

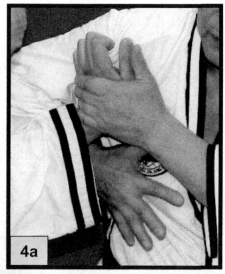

5. Do not lean forward in a slow controlled manner; instead, use quick powerful forward momentum to obtain the lock and to inflict pain.

Upper Sleeve Grab (2)

1. Opponent grabs the upper part of your shirt sleeve.

2. With your left hand reach over and grab the opponent's hand.

3,4. As you lower your body, pull on the opponent's hand to your left while you execute a center knuckle strike to the opponent's armpit.

See the beginning page of Hand Strikes section to see how to form a center knuckle.

Upper Sleeve Grab (2)

5,6,7.   Step diagonally to the left using your right foot and execute a **Kalnukki** to his arm just above the elbow.

Upper Sleeve Grab - Behind (1)

1. Opponent grabs you from behind with both hands grabbing your shirt at the shoulders.

2.   Move your hips to the right side as you tilt your shoulders down to the left.

3, 4.   Immediately move in the opposite direction, tilting your right shoulder down, making sure to roll it counter clockwise. At the same time grab his right hand and deliver a strike to the solar plexus.

Upper Sleeve Grab - Behind (1)

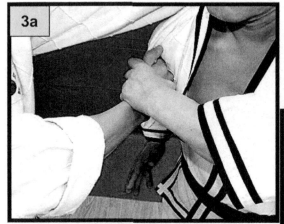

Upper Sleeve Grab - Behind (1)

5,6.   Execute the basic wrist lock. Your left thumb should be on the back of the opponent's hand with the fingers grabbing the inner part of the palm. Your right palm is on the back of the opponent's hand.

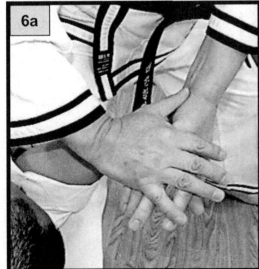

Be sure to get it at a 45 degree angle and drive down on the opponent's wrist.

Upper Sleeve Grab - Behind (2)

1. Opponent grabs your shirt from behind in the upper sleeve area.

2,3.   As you slide to your left, roll your right shoulder in a slight downward clockwise motion.
At the same time grab the opponent's right hand with your left hand.

3.   Grab his hand so that your thumb is pressed against the back of his hand. Immediately use the right shoulder to press against the back of his hand for a wrist lock.

You are using the shoulder instead of the hand to complete the wrist lock.

Upper Sleeve Grab - Behind (2)

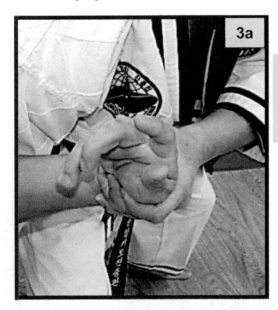

4,5.   After the initial wrist break, follow up by bringing your right hand under his arm and grabbing the opponent on the back of his hand.

Now you should have the opponent under control, while you are in a comfortable sideways stance.

Mid Sleeve Grab – Behind (1)

1. Opponent grabs the middle part of your sleeves near the elbows.

2. Slide to your left as you swing your left arm up and swing your right arm down.

3. Continue to slide your right foot back as you duck under your opponent's left arm.

Mid Sleeve Grab – Behind (1)

4. Trap the opponent's left wrist between your forearm and bicep. Place your right forearm (knife edge) above his elbow.

5. Step forward with your right foot and execute a knife hand strike to the elbow.

6. Keep your opponent's left hand trapped tight against your chest while applying downward pressure on the elbow, **Kalnukki.**

Mid Sleeve Grab – Behind (2)

1. Opponent grabs your shirt at the elbows from behind.

2.   Step back to the left at a 45 degree angle with the left leg.

3.   Immediately bring your right leg behind the opponent's legs and place your left hand behind his left knee. Bring your right elbow up to his chest or solar plexus.

Your upper body has to be slightly tilted to the side in order to facilitate executing this technique.

Mid Sleeve Grab – Behind (2)

4.   Simultaneously pull up with your left hand while you push down with your elbow as you twist your body to the right and drop down to one knee.

In this photo, Grandmaster Kim's left knee is on the ground and the right knee is up to support the opponent's body.

5.   Violently strike down on the opponent's chest or solar plexus with your elbow.

Even when you are striking down with your elbow, keep a "LIVE" hand.

Mid Sleeve Grab – Behind (3)

1. Opponent grabs you at mid-sleeve from behind.

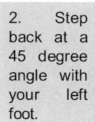

2. Step back at a 45 degree angle with your left foot.

3. Lean forward and grab the opponent's ankle with both hands.

4. Now pull up on their ankle with both of your hands while you squat down on his knee with your behind.

Mid Sleeve Grab – Behind (3)

5. Pay close attention to the hand transition on the foot. Twist his foot outward by pulling up by the side of his heel while pushing down on the toes.

6. As you twist the ankle, turn your body in a clockwise motion. Your right foot should be right behind the opponent's knee. Once you turn around, you should be pushing on the opponent's foot.

7. Use your hands and your body weight to apply pressure on the opponent's ankle and calf.

Shirt Grabs

옷 잡혔을 때
(oht jahp peuht seul tteh)

Shirt Grab – Shoulder (1)

1. Opponent grabs your shirt on your shoulder.

2. Firmly press on the opponent's hand with your left hand.

3. Raise your right hand straight up.

4. As you step forward with your right foot, bring down your right arm in a big "U" motion.

Shirt Grab – Shoulder (1)

5,6.　　　You are securing his wrist in your armpit to execute the wrist lock. Note the 45 degree angle of the opponent's wrist and hand.

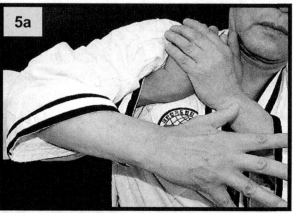

Shirt Grab – Shoulder (2)

1. Opponent grabs your shirt on the shoulder.

2.   With your left hand firmly press on his hand.

3,4.   Bring your right hand to support your left hand and step forward with your right foot.

5.   Lean your body forward and down in a 45 degree angle.

All these techniques are executed with speed, power, and decisiveness.

Shirt Grab – Behind Neck (1)

1. Opponent grabs the back of your shirt collar..

2. Step forward with your right foot, placing it between your opponent's legs. At the same time grab your opponent's belt, pants, or whatever they may be wearing.

3. Now pull on the belt as you thrust your right palm up to their chin.

Shirt Grab – Behind Neck (1)

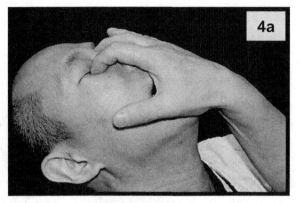

4, 4a, 5. Then dig your fingers into the opponent's eyes.

Shirt Grab – Behind Neck (2)

1. Opponent grabs the back of your shirt collar.

2,3.　　Bring your right palm up to the opponent's elbow and place your left hand over your right hand.

Shirt Grab – Behind Neck (2)

5.   Turn his elbow so that it is facing up.

6,7.   Step back with your left foot and quickly apply pressure to the elbow.

Shirt Grab – Armpit (1)

1. Opponent grabs your shirt just underneath your armpit.

2. With your left hand, grab the opponent on his wrist, just above the base of the palm.

3. Place the knife edge of your right forearm on the inside of his wrist bone.

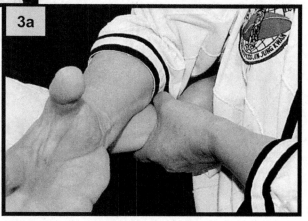

Shirt Grab – Armpit (1)

4. Sharply press down on the pressure point to get your opponent's upper body down in front of you.

5. As his head gets close to you bring your right forearm in front of his throat.

6. Then in a scissor motion slice the opponent's throat by sliding your left hand to the right side and your right hand to the left side.

Shirt Grab – Armpit (2)

1. Opponent grabs your shirt just underneath your armpit.

2. Bring the palm of your right hand nice and tight against your chest. This should trap the opponent's hand at the bend of your arm.

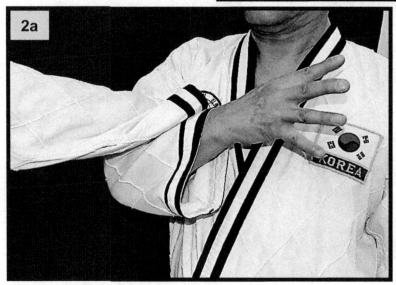

Shirt Grab – Armpit (2)

3. Take a small step back with your left foot.

4,5. Keeping your right arm tight against your chest, execute a side kick to your opponent.

Shirt Grab – Front (1)

1. Opponent grabs you by the front of your shirt.

2.　　Cover his hand with your left hand as you pull it in close and tight to your chest.

3.　　With your right hand grab the opponent just above his wrist.

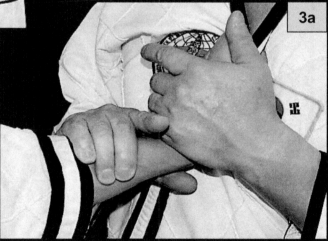

Shirt Grab – Front (1)

4.   Step forward with your right foot and turn your body sideways, bringing the elbow up and over his arm.

Bring your elbow over until the opponent's arm is directly underneath your armpit.

5, 6.   Pull back on the opponent's elbow so that it is bent, and tilt your upper body down at a 45 degree angle, applying pressure on your opponent's wrist.

Shirt Grab – Front (2)

1. Opponent grabs the front of your chest with a closed fist.

2.   Step forward diagonally to the left with your right foot. At the same time, grab the opponent's hand with your left hand. Your left thumb should be on the back of his hand and fingers are grabbing the inside meaty part of his palm.

As you step forward, grab the opponent's bicep pressure point just above the elbow.

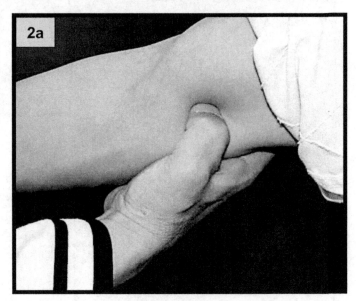

Shirt Grab – Front (2)

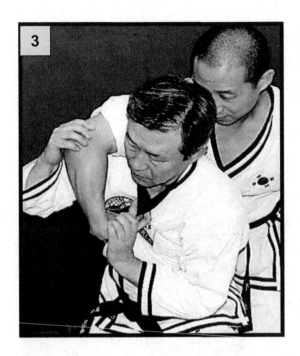

3,4.   Lift his elbow as you step forward and under it.

As you step through, bend his wrist inward.

5.   Once you have his arm behind him, keep pushing his arm while pressing against the wrist. This will put pressure on his shoulder and wrist.

Shirt Grab – Front (3)

1. Opponent grabs your shirt in a closed underhand grip.

2. Grab the opponent's hand with your left hand. Your left thumb is placed on the back of his hand while the rest of the fingers are grabbing the inside meaty part of his palm.

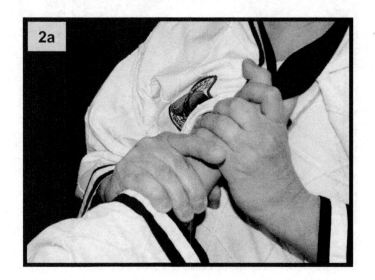

Shirt Grab – Front (3)

3.   With your right hand grab him at the wrist

4.   Now step forward with your right foot and immediately swing your left foot back counter clockwise.   Use the momentum of the swing to torque the opponent's wrist.

Shirt Grab – Front (4)

1. Opponent grabs the front of your shirt with an underhand grip.

2. Grab the opponent's wrist with your right hand, and place your left palm over the length of his thumb.

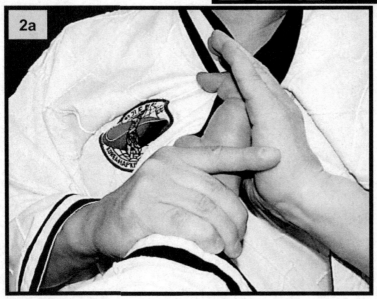

Shirt Grab – Front (4)

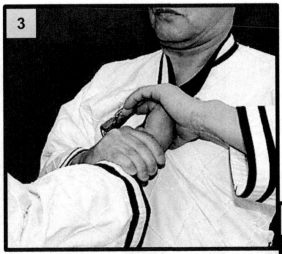

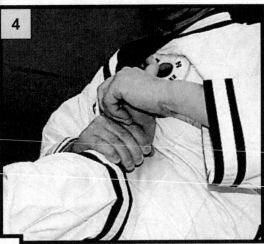

3,4,5.   Push down and out on his thumb to break the grip.

The fingers of your left hand should remain close and tight. This will facilitate in pushing down the opponent's thumb.

Shirt Grab - Behind – Neck (1)

1.   Opponent grabs the collar from behind.

2.   Turn into the grab so that your body is in center line with his.

3.   Place the left foot between the opponent's legs as you grab his belt with the right hand. Strike his chin with an open palm.

4.   Pull with your right hand as you push his head back with your left. You can inflict further pain by poking his eyes with your fingers.

Joint Locks
호신술

Belt Grabs
허리띠 잡혔을 때
(huh rhi tti jahp peuht seul tteh)

Belt Grab – Overhand Grip (1)

1. Opponent grabs your belt in an overhand grip.

2. Grab his hand with your left while you grab the wrist with your right hand.

2a. Leave a space of one index finger between your hands.

3. Pull up with both hands to bend his wrist.

Belt Grab – Overhand Grip (1)

4. At the same time execute a side kick while still holding on to your opponent's hand.

5. After the strike, bring your foot down into a horse stance and initiate a wrist lock by pulling with your left hand while pushing down with the right.

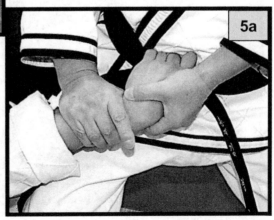

Belt Grab – Overhand Grip (2)

1. Opponent grabs your belt in an overhand grip.

2, 3.   With a "LIVE" hand, pull up on the opponent's wrist with your left forearm.

Be sure to keep your left hand tight against your chest.

Belt Grab – Overhand Grip (2)

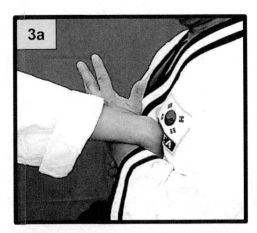

4, 5. Step forward diagonally to the left with your right foot. As you step in bring your right forearm knife hand to the opponent's elbow pressure point to execute a "**Kalnukki**" to the pressure point just above his elbow.

Belt Grab – Overhand Grip (3)

1. Opponent grabs your belt in an overhand grip.

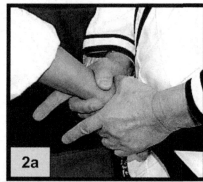

2. Grab the opponent's hand with both your hands. Place your right thumb above your left thumb with the index fingers pointed down.

3. Step diagonally to your left and twist his wrist up at a 45 degree angle. This will release his grip on your belt.

Belt Grab – Overhand Grip (3)

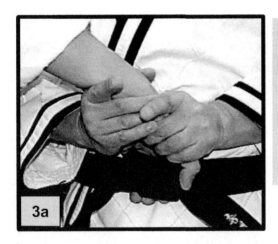

3a

3a. It is important to twist the wrist in a 45 degree angle. You are basically hyper-extending the thumb side of the wrist by pushing up at the wrist while pulling down on the hand. It is important here that you do not bend the wrist inward or outward.

4. Continue to twist so that the opponent will release his grip.

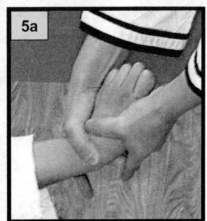

5. Now force him to the floor by continuing the hyperextension.

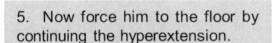

5

Belt Grab – Overhand Grip (4)

1. Opponent grabs your belt in an overhand grip.

2. Step diagonally to the left as you grab his hand with both of yours.

Both index fingers should be pointing straight down and both of your thumbs are right on his wrist, nice and tight.

Belt Grab – Overhand Grip (5)

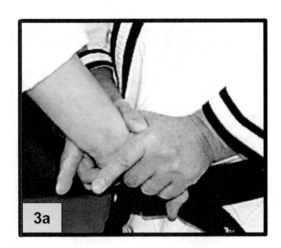

4,5. As you torque his wrist to your left, bend your knees and drive in diagonally with your right shoulder so that it is directly under your opponent's armpit.

Bring your right foot through into a horse stance and pull down on your opponent's arm as you rise up just a bit to hyperextend the arm.

Use caution when practicing this technique. If you do not pay close attention during the execution of this technique there is a strong possibility of injuring your partner.

Belt Grab – Underhand Grip (1)

1. Opponent grabs your belt with an underhand grip.

2, 2a. Step diagonally to the right with your left foot. At the same time, use both of your hands to grab the opponent's wrist.

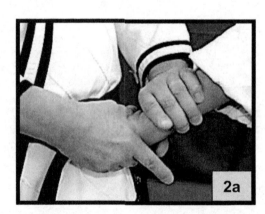

3. Swing your right foot around in a clockwise motion and pull the opponent's wrist close to the left side of your hip in an inverted fashion so that his palm is facing outward and the back of the wrist is firmly secured on your hip.

Belt Grab – Underhand Grip (1)

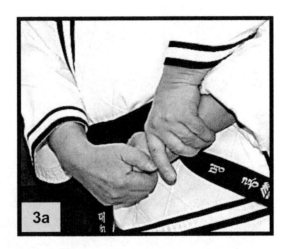

4.   Finish the move by pulling upward on his hand with your right hand while pushing down on the wrist with your left hand.

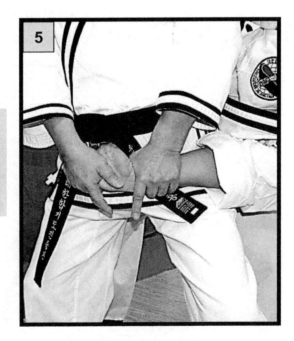

The wrist needs to be straight so that when you pull up and push down with your hands it has the intended effect .

Belt Grab – Underhand Grip (2)

1. Opponent grabs your belt with an underhand grip.

2, 2a.   Step forward with your left foot. At the same time, grab the opponent's wrist with your right hand. Notice how GM Kim grabs the wrist in the picture below. Use the bone next to your knuckle by the index finger and press down on the wrist pressure point (three finger width from the wrist bone, on the inside part of the bone).

As you do that, pull on his elbow towards you with your left hand. You should be pushing down at a 45 degree angle with your right hand while pulling with your left hand.

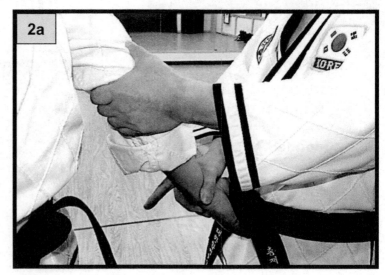

Belt Grab – Underhand Grip (2)

3. Now, drive your right shoulder under the opponent's elbow by lowering your body just enough to get under his arm. Be sure to get close enough to the opponent's body. If you create too much space between you and the opponent, you will have a very difficult time flipping him.

4,5. Once your shoulder is firmly in place, straighten your knees and lower the torso to flip him over.

Basic Punch
Blocking Exercises

막기 기본 10개 동작
(mahk ghi ghi bohn yal geh dohng jahk)

This is an exercise in hand-eye coordination, especially when practicing with a partner. Start out nice and slow and then increase the speed as you get better and more comfortable with the exercise. Remember, these are actual blocks you are practicing, so put power into the blocks just seconds before the actual block. Do not waste any unnecessary energy by applying full power to your arms throughout the entire exercise.

Blocking Exercises

Starting stance is in the neutral stance.

1a. Step forward with you left foot.

At same time bring your left arm down in front of you and bring your right hand down to waist level. Both hands are clenched in a fist.

1b. Quickly raise your left arm for a head block. The arm should be bent at the elbow at a near 90 degree angle. As you block, drive your right fist forward as if to strike an opponent in the gut.

2a. Swing the arms down and execute the same block/ punch move in the opposite direction. Block with the right while punching with the left.

Blocking Exercises

2b,3a. From the face block swing the arm out to the right and swipe it across your face for an inside face block.

3b. Be sure to bring it straight across the front of your face.

4a. Now move your right arm across your face, back to the right for an outside face block.

Blocking Exercises

4b. Your fist should be facing out and your arm should be almost at a 90 degree angle.

4b

5a

5a. Now turn your wrist in so that the palm is facing you and bring it down for an inward down block.

5b

6a

6a. Raise your hand back up slightly (fist at face level).

Blocking Exercises

6b. Bring it down in a closed fist into an outward down block.

7a. Keeping your right hand in place, raise your left hand and bring it down in an inward circular motion for an outward down block.

8a. Keeping your left hand in place, repeat the outward down block with the right arm.

Blocking Exercises

9a. Bend your arms and bring them together in preparation for a double overhead block.

9b. Punch up and out with your forearms bent slightly at the elbow.

Blocking Exercises

10a, 10b. Bring both hands together at chest level before thrusting them all the way down for a double down block. Be sure to thrust down and out with strong, clenched fists.

10a

10b

11

11. Back to original standing position.

Basic Punch

Redirection

방권술

(bahng gwun sool)

Basic Punch Redirection (1)

1. Start position is in a neutral stance.

2,3.   As the punch comes in, step forward with your left foot. Use your left hand (with open palm) to redirect his punch by guiding it past your face.

Maintain eye contact with your opponent.

Basic Punch Redirection (2)

1. Starting position is in the neutral stance.

2,3. Using an open hand palm, step in with your right foot and redirect the punch away from your face.

If you anticipate the punch and block too soon you are liable to get hit.

If you are too late in blocking the punch, you are liable to get hit.

Timing is essential. Anticipate the punch and time the block accordingly. This comes only with practice.

Basic Punch Redirection (3)

1. Starting position is in the neutral stance.

2,3.   Using a knife hand, redirect the incoming punch with the back of your right hand as you step in with your left foot.

3.   You are using the back of your hand instead of the palm to guide the punch past your face.

Basic Punch Redirection (4)

1. Starting position is in a neutral stance.

2,3. Step in with your left foot. Using a knife hand, redirect the incoming punch.

Basic Punch Redirection (5)

1. Starting position is in a neutral stance.

2,3.   Take a small step back with your right foot as the punch comes in. Defend against the punch by cupping his fist and pushing it down.

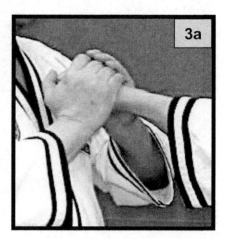

Basic Punch Redirection (6)

1. Start position is in the neutral stance.

2,3. Step forward with your left foot.
Execute an "X" block. With clenched fists, form an "X" and thrust it upward at a 45 degree angle to block the attack.

289

Basic Punch Redirection (7)

1. Starting position is in the neutral stance.

2,3. Step forward with your left foot. Bend your right arm, with the elbow raised higher than the wrist. Cup your hand to redirect the punch.

Elbow is raised to keep the punch in its place instead of having it drop down to the side.

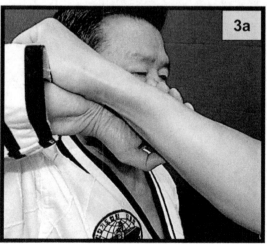

Basic Punch Redirection (8)

1. Starting position is in the neutral stance.

2,3. Using the same cupping motion as the basic punch block (7), step in with your right foot and redirect the punch with your left hand.

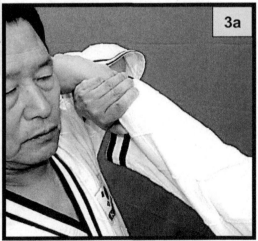

Punch Defenses-

방권술 (bahng gwun sool)

Joint Locks

꺽기 (kkuhk kki)

Strikes

치기 (chi ghi)

Throws

던지기 (duhn ji ghi)

Punch Defense (1)

1. Begin in a neutral stance.

2.

2,3. Step in with your left foot. Redirect the punch using redirection # 8.

3.

4.

4,5. Step forward diagonally with your left foot and execute a **"Kalnukki"** to the pressure point just above his elbow.

5.

Punch Defense (2)

1. Begin in neutral stance.

2. Step forward with the right foot as the punch comes in.

3. Execute redirection #6.

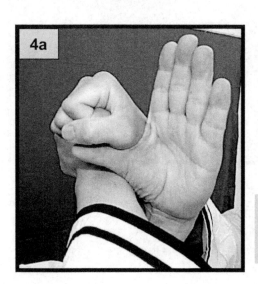

4. As soon as you complete the block, open your left hand, making an "L" shape with your thumb and fingers.

Punch Defense (2)

5. Now swing your opponent's hand down in a clockwise motion until it is at your waist level.

7. Firmly grab the opponent's wrist with your right hand as you push on the back of his hand with your left.

8. Next, execute a kick to your opponent's chest with your left foot.

Punch Defense (3)

1. Begin in a neutral stance.

2,3. As you see the incoming punch, step forward with your right foot and redirect using redirection #8.

Punch Defense (3)

4,5. With a "LIVE" hand, bring your right hand under your opponent's elbow. In a push/pull motion, push downward with your left hand while pulling on his elbow with your right.

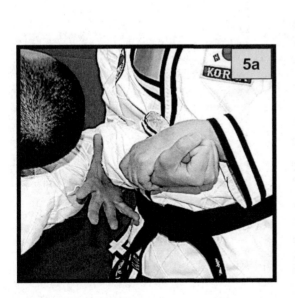

5a. Pull on his elbow with your right "LIVE" hand until his elbow is nearly touching your biceps. This places tremendous pressure on the shoulder joint and is liable to dislocate it if done quickly and forcefully.

Punch Defense (4)

1. Begin in a neutral stance.

2. As the punch comes in, step back slightly with your right foot as you execute redirection #7.

3. After blocking, bring his hand close to your body. Bring your left hand under the opponent's arm and cup your right hand for added support.

4,5. Step diagonally forward with your left foot and execute an arm lock. Remember to have your upper arm firmly against his arm so that the entire weight of your body can by used to execute the move.

Punch Defense (5)

1. Begin in a neutral stance.

2. Step forward with your left foot and bring your left hand up and execute redirection #1.

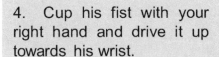

3. Grab his wrist immediately and lower it, bringing it down to waist level.

4. Cup his fist with your right hand and drive it up towards his wrist.

Punch Defense (5)

5. To inflict more pain, squeeze his knuckles as you bend his wrist.

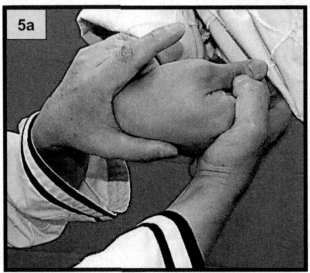

Punch Defense (5)

6,7. Quickly reverse his wrist so it is facing up and drive down hard and quick on his wrist.

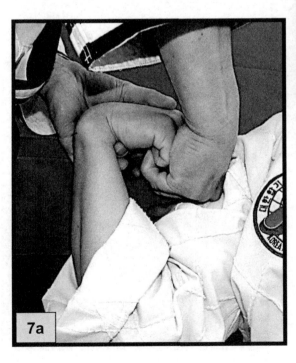

Punch Defense (6)

1. Begin in a neutral stance.

2. Execute redirection #1.

3. As you turn your body to the right slightly, grab the opponent's hand with your left hand. At the same time, bring your right hand and grab the back of his hand.

4. Now bring it around in a counter clockwise motion as you turn your body in the same direction.

Punch Defense (6)

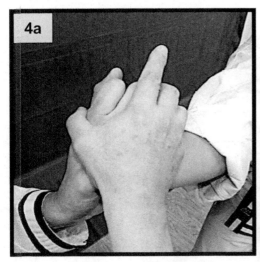

5. Now execute a wrist joint lock at a 45 degree angle.

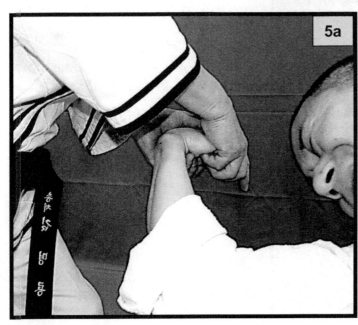

Punch Defense (7)

1. Begin in a neutral stance.

2,3. Using redirection #8, step forward with your right foot and block with your left hand. Your elbow should be at an angle so that it is higher than your hand.

Punch Defense (7)

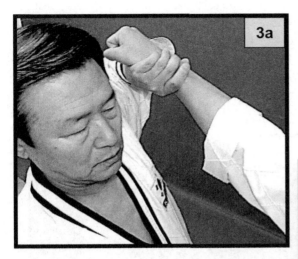

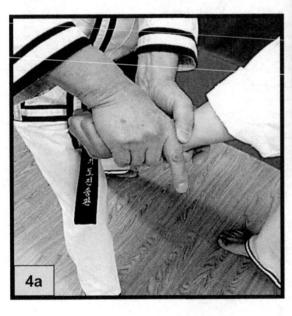

4. With your left hand bring down your opponent's hand in a counter clockwise motion. At the bottom, switch hands, making sure to grab his hand as shown in the picture.

Punch Defense (7)

5,6. Step diagonally to the right with your left foot and go under your opponent's arm. As you step under, bring the right hand down while maintaining the wrist lock.

7. Tuck his hand under the shoulder and immobilize him by pressing on it with your knee.

Punch Defense – Strikes (1)

1. Begin in a neutral stance.

2,3.   Execute redirection #2.

Punch Defense – Strike (1)

4,5. Once you have blocked the incoming punch, immediately attack by striking the opponent on the neck with your knife hand.

5a. Strike the neck at a 45 degree angle with your hands open.

Punch Defense – Strikes (2)

1. Begin in a neutral stance.

2. Execute redirection #2.

3. Grab opponent's wrist and bring it down to your waist level. At the same time, raise your right hand straight up into an open knife hand.

Punch Defense – Strikes (2)

4. Immediately swing your right hand down and strike the opponent's wrist with the knife hand. At the same time, your left hand should be going up as your right hand is coming down.

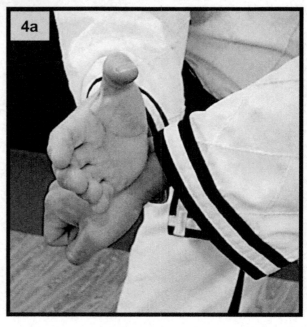

Punch Defense – Strikes (3)

1. Begin in a neutral stance.

2,3. Execute redirection #3.

Punch Defense – Strikes (3)

4. After redirecting the punch, continue to raise your right hand all the way up.

5. Guide his punching hand at a downward angle as you bring down your right knife hand on the back of your opponent's neck.

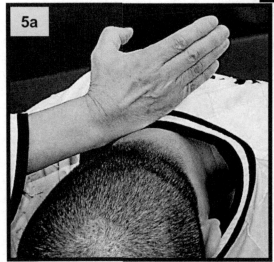

These moves should transition smoothly to end up in one fluid motion.

Punch Defense – Strikes (4)

1. Begin in a neutral stance.

2. Execute redirection #7. Step forward with your right foot and redirect with your left hand.

3,3a. While maintaining a hold on his wrist, lower your body and execute a strike to the solar plexus using the palm of your hand. Strike at a 45 degree upward angle for maximum affect.

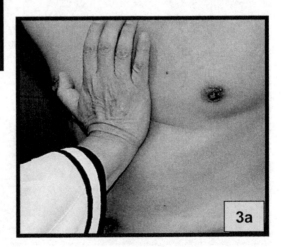

Punch Defense – Strikes (5)

1. Begin in a neutral stance.

2. Execute redirection #2 to redirect the incoming punch. As you redirect, get into a horse stance with your knees bent.

3. After you redirect, bring your right hand back, keeping it open in a knife hand.

Punch Defense – Strikes (5)

Strike the opponent just below the chest, striking upward at a 45 degree angle.

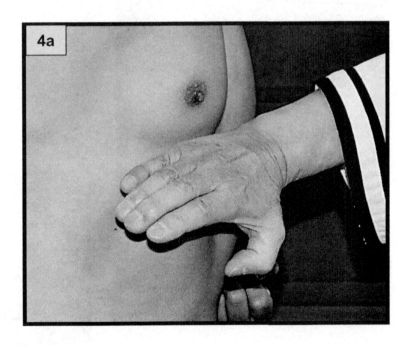

Punch Defense – Strikes (6)

1. Begin in a neutral stance.

2. Execute redirection #2 to redirect the punch. Step forward with your left foot and redirect with an open palm.

3. Maintain a hold of his wrist.

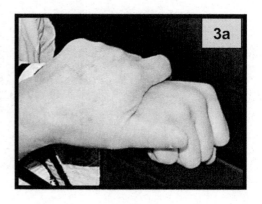

Punch Defense – Strikes (6)

4. Turn your body clockwise and execute an elbow strike to the kidney area.

6, 7. Immediately turn clockwise once more and deliver a punch.

Punch Defense – Strikes (7)

1.
Begin in a neutral stance.

2. Execute redirection #7 to redirect the punch. Step to the left diagonally and redirect with your right hand.

3, 4. While keeping a hold of his wrist, deliver a heel kick to the back of his head.

Punch Defense – Strikes (8)

1. Begin in a neutral stance.

2. As the punch is coming, step diagonally to the left to avoid the attack.

3. Simultaneously deliver a punch to the ribcage using the middle knuckle strike.

4, 5. Immediately follow up the punch with a knife hand strike to the back of the opponent's neck.

Punch Defense – Throws (1)

1. Begin in a neutral stance.

2. Execute redirection #7 to redirect the punch. Step forward with your left foot and redirect with your left hand.

3. Once you have redirected the punch, grab his wrist as you grab his right shoulder with your right hand.

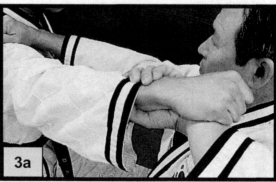

Punch Defense – Throws (1)

4. Use both of your hands to push him backwards as you xecute a kick to the back of his leg to take him to the ground.

Punch Defense – Throws (1)

7, 7a. Once your opponent is on the ground, immediately place your right knee on his elbow as you pull the wrist towards you. This is a very effective way to hyperextend the arm.

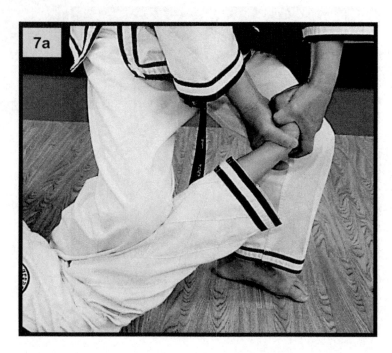

Punch Defense – Throws (2)

1.
Begin in a neutral stance.

2,3.   Execute redirection #7 to redirect the punch. Step forward with your left foot and redirect with your left hand.

Punch Defense – Throws (2)

4. Swing his hand backwards in a wide arch and step in for a hip throw.

5. Make sure the left side of your hip lines up with the right side of his hip as you wrap your right arm across the front of his body.

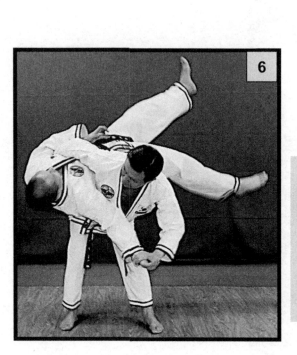

6. In order for this technique to work, it is imperative for you to commit to the move by stepping in as soon as you block the punch. Again, turning the step into one fluid motion is essential to rendering the technique effective.

Punch Defense – Throws (3)

1. Begin in a neutral stance.

2. Execute redirection #7 to redirect the punch. Step forward with your right foot and redirect with your left hand.

3. Grab the opponent's hand and bring it down and grab his hand with your right hand.

4. Your fingers should be grabbing the back of the opponent's hand and your thumb should be grabbing the meaty part of their thumb.

5. Swing your arm clockwise up and over your head while placing your left foot directly behind the opponent's right leg. At the same time place your left arm in between your opponent's legs.

6. In one motion, pull down on his right hand as you hoist his leg. The best way to throw the opponent is to flip him over the small of your back. Keep your knees bent and back slightly arched.

Punch Defense – Throws (4)

1. Begin in a neutral stance.

2. Execute redirection #4. Step forward with your left foot and redirect the punch with your right hand.

3. Continue your forward momentum and slide to his back side, grabbing both of his shoulders at the same time.

4, 5. Pull back on the shoulders as you kick the back of his right knee to force him to the ground.

Punch Defense – Throws (5)

1. Begin in a neutral stance.

2. Execute redirection #1. Step with your left foot and redirect the punch with your left hand.

3. As you step forward, drive your right arm under his, deep towards his neck.

4,5. Strike the opponent's neck with the inside of your forearm. As you do so, step in with your right foot, placing it behind the opponent's left foot. Flip him over the small of your back.

Punch Defense – Throws (6)

1. Begin in a neutral stance.

2. Execute redirection #8. Step forward with your right foot and redirect with your left hand. Your left hand should sort of look like a hook, hooking the opponent's incoming punch.

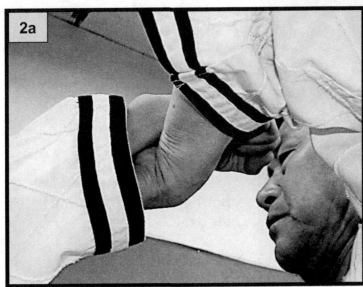

Punch Defense – Throws (6)

3. Grab the opponent's right wrist with your left hand, and at the same time, drive your right arm to the opponent's elbow. His elbow pressure point area should be placed at the bend of your elbow.

4. Pivot on your right foot and swing counter clockwise with your left foot. Push on his wrist with your left hand as you pull inward and upward with your right arm, keeping a "LIVE" hand.

5. Basically, you are hyperextending his arm from the vertical position.

Be sure to keep your hips in line with your opponent's hips and flip him over.

Basic Side Kick and
Heel Kick Blocks
발차기 방어 기술
(bahl cha ghi bahng uh ghi sool)

Basic Side Kick Block (1)

1. Beginning stance is a modified back stance, with the left fist at your waist and right fist at your chest.

2. As the kick comes in, step to the side with your left foot and block the kick with your right closed fist in a downward blocking motion.

As always, maintain eye contact with your opponent.

Basic Side Kick Block (2)

1. Begin in the modified back stance.

2. As the kick comes in, step diagonally forward to the left with your left foot. At the same time block the kick with a downward block with your right closed fist.

Basic Side Kick Block (3)

1. Beginning stance is in a modified back stance.

2. As the kick comes in, step forward with your left foot, keeping your knees bent. At the same time, block the kick with the bottom part of your outer forearm.

Basic Side Kick Block (4)

1. Begin in a modified back stance.

2. As the kick comes in, move your back leg 90 degrees in a counter clockwise motion.

At the same time, block the kick with the outer portion of your right forearm.

Basic Side Kick Block (5)

1. Begin in a modified back stance.

2. As the kick comes in, lean your body slightly forward and thrust your crossed arms down on the opponent's leg. Your wrists should be right on top of each other as you execute the "X" block.

The best way to execute this block is to use a short thrust at a downward angle AS THE KICK COMES IN.

Basic Side Kick Block (6)

1. Begin in a modified back stance.

2. As the kick comes in curve your hands and "cup" the opponent's leg by placing your left hand on top and your right hand on the bottom.

3. Close your hands on the calf and slide your hands back until you get to the ankles.

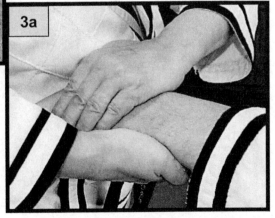

Basic Side Kick Block (7)

1. Begin in a modified back stance.

2. As the kick comes in, execute a down block with your right hand.

3. Immediately slide both of your hands (palms facing up) underneath the leg as you get into a side horse stance.

Heel Kick Block

1. Begin in a modified back stance.

2. As the heel kick comes in, step out to the side with your left foot. At the same time, grip your right hand with your left and bend your right arm at a 90 degree angle. Lean your body toward the kick as you block it.

Be sure to have your right forearm directly in front of your face to have a solid block.

Defense Against Side Kick
and Roundhouse Kick

옆차기 / 찍어차기 방어
(yup cha ghi / jjick uh cha ghi bahng uh)

Side Kick Defense (1)

1. Begin in a modified back stance.

2. As the kick comes in, step forward diagonally and block the kick with your right arm.

3. Immediately after the block, hook your arm under the leg and pull it tight close to your chest.

341

Side Kick Defense (1)

4,5.   Now execute a **"Kalnukki"** to the thigh.

Be sure to press down quick and hard on the thigh for maximum effect.

Side Kick Defense (2)

1. Begin in a modified back stance.

2. As the kick comes in, step forward with your left foot (moving slightly to the left side as you step forward) and block the kick with the outer edge of your left forearm.

3. Immediately wrap your right arm over the leg and pull it in close to your body.

Side Kick Defense (2)

4,5. Slide your left arm to the opponent's thigh and execute a **"Kalnukki"** in one quick motion.

When executing the kalnukki, keep your hand "LIVE" and maintain eye contact with your opponent.

Side Kick Defense (3)

1. Begin in a modified back stance.

2. Execute the basic side kick block #6.

3. Immediately transition your right palm to the top of the foot and place your left hand on the heel.

Side Kick Defense (3)

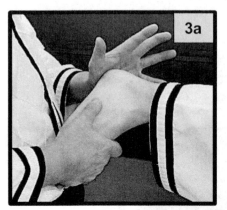

4. As you step back with the right foot, pull up with the right hand as you push down at a 45 degree angle with your left.

Again, this action is executed in a very quick and powerful motion.

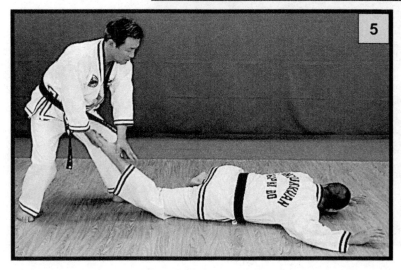

5. Continue with the push/pull until the opponent has dropped to the ground.

Side Kick Defense (3)

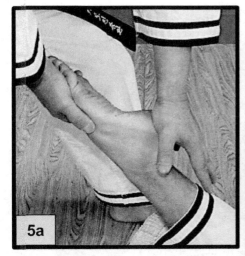

6,7. Once you have him on the ground, wrap your right leg inside the back of his right leg. Place your foot just on the inside of his inner thigh and lower your body so that you are essentially sitting on his shin.

Your shin should be driving down on the back of their thigh as you go down.

Side Kick Defense (4)

Begin in a modified back stance.

2. Execute the basic side kick block #2 and immediately slide your left hand under his leg and place it on the top of his foot.

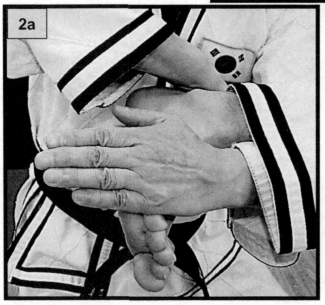

Side Kick Defense (4)

3, 3a.   Immediately grab the blade of his foot with your left hand and place your right palm on the inside of the opponent's heel.

4.   Slightly elevate the leg before pulling it down quickly as you push on the heel and pull on the foot blade. The purpose of elevating the leg is to create more distance to generate greater speed when you pull down on it.

Your opponent should fall to the ground and roll over to relieve the pressure being applied to his ankle.

Side Kick Defense (4)

6,7.   Once he has rolled over, immediately secure his other leg by pressing down on the inner thigh. At the same time, twist his ankle for added pressure.

Side Kick Defense (5)

1. Begin in a modified back stance.

2. Step forward slightly with your right foot and execute the basic side kick block #5 (X-block). Make sure your right wrist is on top of your left wrist.

3. Immediately step out to the side with your left foot and cup his foot and ankle at the bend of your arm.

Side Kick Defense (5)

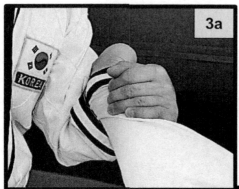

3a. The top of his foot should be firmly secured against your bicep, right at the bend of your elbow, with your left hand grasping the back of the lower calf.

4. Hook the inside of his heel with your right hand.

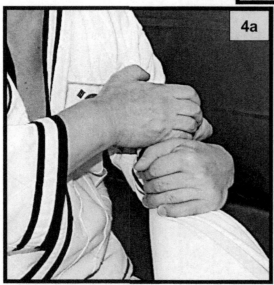

Side Kick Defense (5)

5,6. As you step back with your right foot, pull down at a 45 degree angle on the heel with your right hand in a clockwise circular motion.

7. It is important to pull on the heel as you make the rotation. Separating the motions will hinder the effectiveness of the technique.

Side Kick Defense (5)

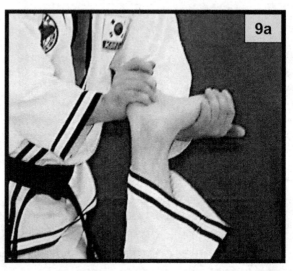

8,9. Once the opponent has flipped over, immediately twist the ankle in the opposite direction and strike down on the left inner thigh with the blade of your right foot.

Side Kick Defense (6)

1. Begin in a modified back stance.

2. When you see the opponent's foot lift up, slide your right foot slightly back and raise your right arm. At the same time bring your left hand up to cover the right side of your ribcage (fingers open and palms facing out).

3. As the opponent is fully extending his kick, strike down hard with your elbow on the side of his foot, just below the ankle.

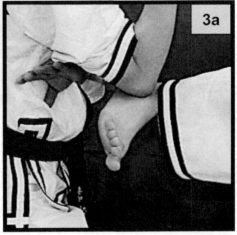

Side Kick Defense (7)

1. Begin in a modified back stance.

2. As the kick comes in, slightly slide your right foot back, cover your ribcage with your left hand, and raise your right hand up to your face level in a closed fist.

3. As the kick is being fully extended, strike down with a back handed fist on his foot (just below the ankle) with your knuckles.

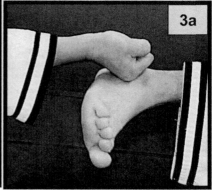

Side Kick Defense (8)

1. Begin in a modified back stance.

2. Execute the block using side kick block #2. Step forward (slightly to the left) with your left foot and block the kick with the outer part of your wrist.

3. Immediately transition your body into a horse stance. At the same time grab the opponent's leg from the bottom and raise your right hand high above you.

Side Kick Defense (8)

4. Strike the opponent's leg as you release the leg.

You want to strike the area just above the ankle with the knife hand.

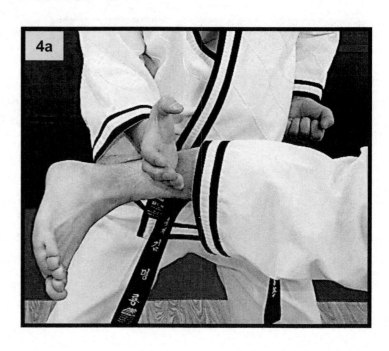

Side Kick Defense (9)

Begin in a modified back stance.

2. When you see the opponent initiating the attack, bring your foot up in order to execute a side kick block.

3. Make sure to lift your leg to at least chest level.

4. Once your foot is up at the 12 o'clock position, turn your foot outward and bring it down hard and fast, striking the opponent on the leg above the ankle.

Side Kick Defense (10)

1. Begin in a modified back stance.

2. Use side kick block #2 to block the incoming kick.

3. Immediately hook your right arm under his leg as you grab his arm to prevent him from any possible attack.

Side Kick Defense (10)

4,5. Quickly execute a low kick to the opponent.

Side Kick Defense (11)

1. Begin in a modified back stance.

2. Use side kick block #3 to block the incoming side kick.

4. Immediately after blocking, step forward a little more with your left foot and execute an elbow strike to the thigh.

Side Kick Defense (12)

1. Begin in a modified back stance.

2. Use side kick block #5 to block this incoming side kick.

3. From the X-block position, grab your opponent's ankle with both of your hands.

Side Kick Defense (12)

4,5. Raise the leg up to chest level and kick the opponent's inner thigh.

Side Kick Defense (13)

1. Begin in modified back stance.

2. Use side kick block #2 to block the incoming side kick.

3. Immediately hook your right arm under his leg and grab his arm with your left hand.

4. Execute an inside crescent kick to the opponent's chest.

Roundhouse Defense (1)

1. Begin in a modified back stance.

2.   Bring your left foot behind your right foot and bring both of your hands up (palms facing out) and block the roundhouse kick.

The block is not a hard, firm block. Instead, it is a soft block to deflect the blow.

3.   Step forward with your right foot and strike the opponent on the neck or temple with your knife hand.

Roundhouse Defense (2)

1. Begin in a modified back stance.

2. Once you see the kick coming, quickly step forward with your right foot and execute a center knuckle punch to the opponent's solar plexus.

Always maintain eye contact with your opponent at all times.

Roundhouse Defense (3)

1. Begin in a modified back stance.

2.   Move your left foot behind your right leg in a sideways motion. At the same time block the kick with your right outer forearm and grab the leg near the ankle with your left hand.

3.   Move your right foot behind your opponent's left leg and grab his shoulder with your right hand.

4.   As you pull back with your right leg, push on the shoulder to take him to the ground.

Roundhouse Defense (4)

1. Begin in a modified back stance.

2. Move your left foot behind your right leg in a sideways motion. At the same time block the roundhouse kick with the outer part of your right forearm and grab the ankle with your left hand.

3. Execute a low side kick to your opponent's left knee with your right foot. The target can be the knee or the inner thigh right above the knee.

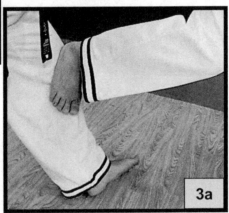

Roundhouse Defense (5)

1. Begin in a modified back stance.

2. As they execute the roundhouse kick, bend your knees and lower your body to avoid the kick.

3. Immediately kick your opponent on the leg just below the knee with the blade of your right foot.

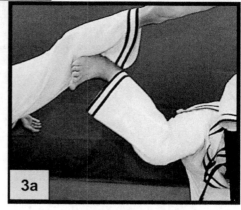

Throwing Techniques Against

던지기 기술 (duhn ji ghi ghi sool)

Wrist Grabs

손목 잡혔을 때 (sohn mohk jahp peuht seul tteh)

Side Kicks

옆차기 (yup cha ghi)

Roundhouse Kicks

찍어차기 (jjick uh cha ghi)

Wrist Grab – Throw (1)

1. As soon as you are grabbed, make your land "LIVE".

2. Step in with your left foot, toes pointed out and knees bent. Turn your body so that your arm and your opponent's arm are parallel to each other.

3. Strike him on the chest with your elbow.

Notice Grandmaster Kim's stance, it is lowered and leaning slightly forward, hips inside the opponent's hips, and the opponent's arm firmly secured on top of his shoulder.

4. Step in with your right foot, placing your right shoulder under his arm (bicep).

Wrist Grab – Throw (1)

5. To throw him, drive up with your legs as you bend over even further, while you pull down on his arm.

7. Once he is on the ground, place your left knee on the side of his jaw and hyperextend his elbow with your hands.

Wrist Grab – Throw (2)

1. As soon as you are grabbed, make your land "LIVE".

2. Step in with your left foot with toes pointed out and knees slightly bent.

3. Release your right wrist and execute a backhand strike to his chest.

4. Reach around to the opponent's back as you step in with your right foot.

Wrist Grab – Throw (2)

5, 6.   Execute the throw and take your opponent to the ground.

7.   As before, immediately press down on his jaw with the left knee while you hyperextend his arm using both of your hands.

Wrist Grab – Throw (3)

1. As soon as you are grabbed, make your hand "LIVE".

2. Step forward with your right foot. Push his hand up and over his shoulder with your right hand.

3. Now step in with your left foot and swing his arm behind his back. Strike his shoulder with your left hand as you bring your left foot behind his left leg.

Out on the streets, you would actually be striking the opponent's throat with your left hand as you move forward; however, we place our hands on the shoulder during practice to prevent accidental injuries.

Wrist Grab – Throw (3)

4,5. Push on the shoulder pull down on his arm while kicking the back of the opponent's leg to take him down.

6. Immediately execute a kick to his solar plexus.

The finishing moves are obviously optional, depending on your specific encounter at the time.

Wrist Grab – Throw (4)

1. As soon as you are grabbed, make your hand "LIVE".

2. Step forward with your left foot as you bend your right arm to pull the opponent in towards you.

3. As you pull him in, grab his arm or shirt at the elbow with your left hand.

Wrist Grab – Throw (4)

5. Pivoting on your left foot, turn clockwise, bending your body at the hips. As you do so, bend his arm at the elbow to facilitate the throw.

This cannot be stressed enough. Your hip placement is extremely important. Notice how GM Kim's hip is aligned with the opponent's hip.

Wrist Grab – Throw (4)

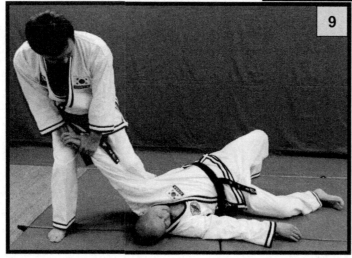

After the throw, maintain control of his arm. As you pull and twist the arm, press down on his elbow using your knee.

Wrist Grab – Throw (5)

1. As soon as you are grabbed, make your hand "LIVE".

2. Take a step forward with your left foot and bend your right arm to pull the opponent towards you.

3. Grab his wrist and lock your left arm behind his arm, just above the elbow. Keeping his arm secure, drive his wrist towards him. This essentially hyperextends his arm from the standing position.

Wrist Grab – Throw (5)

5, 6. Pivoting on your left foot, turn clockwise making sure to place your foot right in front of the opponent's. Now, bend your body at the waist and throw him over.

Wrist Grab – Throw (5)

After the throw, maintain control of his arm and execute the same elbow lock as in Wrist Grab – Throw 4.

Wrist Grab – Throw (6)

1. As soon as you are grabbed, make your hand "LIVE".

2. Bending your left knee, step forward and grab the back of his wrist with your left hand. Pull it towards you as you press forward on his fingers with the knife edge of your right hand.

Wrist Grab – Throw (6)

3. Place your right foot against the back of his left leg and slip your right arm between his legs. Simultaneously, hyperextend his left arm by pulling it down your side.

4,5. Continue pulling down on his left arm as you lift him up with your right arm to execute the throw.

Cross Hand Grab – Throw (1)

1. As soon as you are grabbed, make your hand "LIVE".

2. Step forward with your left foot. Grab his right hand with your left and twist his hand outward to free yourself from his grasp.

3, 3a, 4, 5. Now, step forward with your right foot as you wrap your right arm around his body. Place your hip behind his hip and execute the throw.

Cross Hand Grab – Throw (1)

6. Upon execution, maintain control of his arm. Press down on his neck with your left knee while bending his wrist to apply pressure.

Cross Hand Grab – Throw (2)

1. As soon as you are grabbed, make your hand "LIVE".

2. Raise his hand by applying pressure on his wrist using your thumb and index finger. Your other 3 fingers are grabbing the back of his hand.

3. Swing his arm down and out to your right as you step in with the right foot.

4. Follow through with the left foot and wrap your left arm around the opponent's back. Lean forward and execute the throw by pulling on his right arm and thrusting your hips upward.

Cross Hand Grab – Throw (2)

4a. Pull on his arm against your body to hyperextend it.

6,7. After the throw, grab his left arm and apply pressure under his jaws with your foot while pulling and twisting on his arm.

Cross Hand Grab – Throw (3)

1. As soon as you are grabbed, make your hand "LIVE".

2. Raise his hand by applying pressure on his wrist using your thumb and index finger. Your other 3 fingers are grabbing the back of his hand.

3. Pull his arm down quickly as you step forward with your right foot and place your left palm against his elbow. You are pushing down with your right hand and pulling up with your left to hyperextend his elbow.

Cross Hand Grab – Throw (3)

4,5.   Step in with your left foot and position his arm over your shoulder. As you pull down on his arm, thrust your hips up and execute the throw.

Once you have him on the ground, take action to further control him.

Two Handed Wrist Grab - Throw

1. As soon as you are grabbed, make your hands "LIVE".

2. Step forward with your left foot. Twist your right hand to the outside and bring it up to the front of his face. Place your left hand behind his right knee.

3, 4. Drive forward with the right hand as you pull on the leg with your left to execute the throw.

Two Handed Wrist Grab - Throw

5, 5a. Once your opponent is on the ground, you can finish with a toe kick to his solar plexus.

Both Wrist Grab – Throw (1)

1. As soon as you are grabbed, make your hands "LIVE".

2. This technique is identical to the two handed wrist grab throw technique. Step forward with your left foot, twist your right hand to the outside and bring it up to the front of his face. Place your left hand behind his right knee.

3. Pull on his leg as you drive him down with your right hand to make him fall to the ground.

Both Wrist Grab – Throw (1)

You can finish off the opponent with a final kick to the solar plexus.

Both Wrist Grab – Throw (2)

1. As soon as you are grabbed, make your hands "LIVE".

2. Swing both of your hands to the right to divert your opponent's power. Keep your arms slightly bent so that your opponent's body sways forward.

3. Immediately swing your arms in the opposite direction as you step in with the left foot with knees bent and body lowered. As you do this, firmly grasp both of his wrists with your hands, criss-crossing his arms so that his right arm is on top of his left arm.

Both Wrist Grab – Throw (2)

4. Now step forward with your right foot and place your body in front of his in order to execute the throw.

4a. Notice that your opponent's left elbow is on top of your right shoulder. This facilitates in hyperextending the arm as you execute the throw.

Both Wrist Grab – Throw (2)

5,6.   As you pull down on his arms quickly, straighten your legs to thrust up your hips and throw your opponent to the ground.

7.   Maintain control of his arm by thrusting your foot (jok do) on his neck/jaw as you pull and twist his arm.

Shirt Grab - Behind – Neck (3)

1. Opponent grabs your collar from behind.

2. As you step back slightly with your left foot, pull down on your opponent's elbow with your left hand.

3. As you bring your right foot back into a flipping position, use your right forearm to strike the opponent on the side of the neck.

Shirt Grab - Behind – Neck (3)

4, 5. After the strike, continue to wrap around his neck and use the momentum to flip him over.

Belt Grab – Overhand Grip (4)

1. Opponent grabs your belt with an overhand grip.

2. Grab the opponent's wrist with your right hand. Grab the opponent on the middle part of the sleeve or the elbow (if they are wearing short sleeve) with your left hand. Step diagonally to the right with the left foot.

Belt Grab – Overhand Grip (4)

3,4. Swing your right foot back clockwise and toss him over your shoulder.

Your knees should be slightly bent and your back not too far from his chest. Having too much space between you and the opponent makes it that much more difficult for you to throw your opponent.

Side Kick Defense – Throw (1)

1. Begin in a modified back stance.

2.   The moment your opponent executes a side kick, step forward with your left foot, grabbing the ankle with your right hand and blocking his leg with your left forearm.

3.   With both of your hands firmly grabbing his leg, pull it close to your body.

4.   As you circle your right leg clockwise, extend your left leg out in order to catch his left leg.

Side Kick Defense – Throw (1)

5,6,7,8.   At the full twist of your upper body, fully extend your left leg and trip your opponent, taking him to the ground.

Side Kick Defense – Throw (1)

9. Now quickly place your right foot on the inside of his right thigh.

10. Once your leg is interlocked with his, press down on it using your body weight. Continue with the pressure on his toes for added pain.

Side Kick Defense – Throw (2)

1. Begin in a modified back stance.

2. The moment your opponent executes a side kick, step forward with your left leg and trap his leg by the ankle between your right forearm and bicep.

3. Grab his shirt/arm with your left hand and slide towards your opponent.

Side Kick Defense – Throw (2)

4,5,6. As you pull down on his arm/shirt, sweep his leg from underneath him using your left foot and take him to the ground.

Side Kick Defense – Throw (3)

1. Begin in a modified back stance.

2. The moment your opponent executes a side kick, step forward with your left leg into horse stance and place both of your hands (palms up) under his leg.

Side Kick Defense – Throw (3)

3,4,5.   Quickly lift his legs up in an arc as you take another quick step forward and force him to the ground.

Roundhouse Defense – Throw (1)

1. Begin in a modified back stance.

2.   The moment your opponent executes a roundhouse kick, step in by sliding your left leg behind your right. At the same time, block the kick just above his knee with your right forearm blade and use an overhand hook to grab the base of his leg.

Roundhouse Defense – Throw (1)

3.   As you grab his right upper arm/shirt, slide your right leg behind his left to execute a sweep.

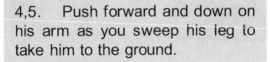

4,5.   Push forward and down on his arm as you sweep his leg to take him to the ground.

Roundhouse Defense – Throw (2)

1. Begin in a modified back stance.

2. The initial roundhouse block is the same as Roundhouse Defense – Throw 1.

Roundhouse Defense – Throw (2)

3.   Grab his leg with both hands using a overhand hook grip as you slide in and execute a leg sweep.

4.   Be sure to turn your body to the left as you extend your right leg for the sweep.

5.   Once he is on the ground, thrust the blade of your foot on his inner thigh and press on the shin with your forearm blade.

We hope you gained additional insight in Hapkido techniques than when you first picked up this book. As stated before, practice makes perfect, so strive to continue your practice of these techniques on your own or with a partner. If at all possible, find a well qualified instructor in your area to assist you in perfecting these techniques.

Also, as you practice, you will inevitably find that you favor some techniques over other techniques, which is perfectly fine. You should practice your favorite techniques repeatedly so that you will be able to execute those techniques flawlessly every single time, essentially becoming "one" with the technique.

We sincerely thank you for purchasing this instructional book. Hopefully, we will be putting forth additional Jin Jung Kwan Hapkido book(s) in the near future. ***"Jin Jung!"***

Printed in Great Britain
by Amazon

46114751R00231